Advance Praise for
The Unwritten Rules of the Game

"An extraordinarily clear depiction of organizational nuances and the emotions that drive the corporate world. A fast-paced, well-developed look at the corporate ladder and the people that climb it. A fascinating depiction of the corporate animal in all of its colors."

—LES MCCRAW, Chairman and CEO, Fluor Corporation

"Peter Scott-Morgan's book is not about organizational or management theory; it is about basic human behavior in the workplace, written in easy to understand terms ... Worth reading before the next organizational change; it will help get the effective results *you* want."

—ROBERT C. STEMPEL, former Chairman and CEO of General Motors

"Finally ... a book that takes the mumbo-jumbo and mystique out of corporate culture. *Unwritten Rules* provides a practical way to search-out and destroy the hidden barriers to high performance that plague companies worldwide. It is a key prerequisite to any successful rethinking of a business's basics."

—ROBERT M. TOMASKO, author of *Rethinking the Corporation* and *Downsizing*

"Scott-Morgan has put his finger on a most important underlying reality of organizational life. Every manager should become familiar with his 'unwritten rules of the game' analysis."

—ROBERT LEVERING, coauthor of *The 100 Best Companies to Work for in America* and *A Great Place to Work*

"Scott-Morgan offers a tough-minded look at what may be the toughest job of all: making positive changes in large organizations ... If you're looking for another dose of feel-good inspiration, this book isn't for you. If you want uncommon sense about the real work of change, you've come to the right place."

—WILLIAM TAYLOR, Founding Editor, *Fast Company*

"Peter Scott-Morgan has given people who want to break free of the tyranny of the all-devouring unwritten rules a way of fighting back. If enough people actually get rule-busting, there is even a fighting chance of creating organizations where people are lead, not just managed, and of a decent future for human enterprise."

—ILFRYN PRICE, **former head of process review, British Petroleum**

"This book is different. This book is the antidote to those fashionable organizational change initiatives of recent years which have frequently failed to impress ... don't be surprised if it becomes the management book of the 1990s."

—LYNDA GRATTON, **London Business School**

"If you think your business is perfectly poised to succeed in the years ahead, don't bother to read this book. But, if you truly want to rise to the challenges of the '90s, you can't afford to let *The Unwritten Rules of the Game* pass you by."

—WILLIAM L. BOYAN, **President and COO, John Hancock Mutual Life Insurance Company**

The Unwritten Rules
of the Game

Master Them, Shatter Them,
and Break Through
the Barriers to Organizational Change

Peter Scott-Morgan

McGraw-Hill, Inc.

New York   San Francisco   Washington, D.C.   Auckland   Bogotá
Caracas   Lisbon   London   Madrid   Mexico City   Milan
Montreal   New Delhi   San Juan   Singapore
Sydney   Tokyo   Toronto

Library of Congress Cataloging-in-Publication Data

Scott-Morgan, Peter.
    The unwritten rules of the game : master them, shatter them, and break through the barriers to organizational change / Peter Scott-Morgan.
       p.   cm.
   ISBN 0-07-057075-2 (alk. paper)
   1. Organizational change. I. Title.
HD58.8.S42 1994
658.4'06—dc20
                                            94-4722
                                             CIP

1 2 3 4 5 6 7 8 9 0 DOC/DOC 9 0 9 8 7 6 5 4

ISBN 0-07-057075-2

The sponsoring editor for this book was Philip Ruppel, the editing supervisor was Fred Dahl, and the production supervisor was Suzanne Babeuf. It was set in Baskerville by Inkwell Publishing Services.

Printed and bound by R. R. Donnelley & Sons Company.

This book is printed on recycled, acid-free paper containing a minimum of 50 percent recycled de-inked fiber.

*Gifts from the four most influential people in my life
made it almost inevitable that one day I would write this book.
In return, the least I can do is dedicate it to them, with love and thanks.*

*To **Mar**, who showed me how to feel what others feel.
To **Da**, who taught me to decipher chaos through reason.
To **Rob**, who encouraged me to rebel against injustice.
And, above all, to **Francis**, who inspired me to believe that you can
take on the world
and win.*

Contents

Acknowledgments

"It would be so great if you could write a book on the unwritten rules of the game," they said. "Really, the sooner the better," they said. "But we know you don't have any spare time."

"I suppose I could always squeeze it in over weekends," I offered. "But it might take a year ..."

No one could have been more surprised than I was when five weekends later I had finished writing the book. "Well done!" they said. "Guess it couldn't have been so difficult," they said. "After all, it didn't take long and you didn't need help."

"Ah," I replied, "but have you any idea how long it took, and how many people helped me, to get to the stage in which I *could* write the book in five weekends ... ?"

Five years and hundreds of people. I have been immensely fortunate to spend the past eight years in what is probably the most supportive international consulting company in the world–Arthur D. Little, Inc. Free from the rigidity that would have been imposed on me elsewhere, I was encouraged to develop my embryonic ideas, even though the business community had not yet focused on barriers to change. It would have been all too easy for my very busy colleagues just to leave the whole idea alone. Instead, key individuals at Arthur D. Little actively encouraged and helped me. Importantly, they had faith in my belief that we all needed to learn how to address the "soft" side of business in a pragmatic way. And they maintained that faith even at times when I was close to giving up.

During that period, a large number of my colleagues, and then an even larger number of clients, acted as sounding boards for my ideas. Refusing to allow the least sloppiness in my thinking, they asked the toughest questions, and as a result, they improved the concepts immeasurably. By the early '90s, when organizations started to recognize that they were running up against hidden barriers to change, the Unwritten Rules of the Game methodology was ready and waiting. And suddenly we were at the cutting edge of thinking on the subject.

But it is no accident that the Unwritten Rules of the Game approach was developed at Arthur D. Little. For more than a century the company has attracted special people who together have created a special culture. Over the last few years, several of those special people have gone above and beyond the call of duty to help and support me often when there was nothing in it for them but extra hassle.

Special mention goes to Isobel and Kathleen for teaching me to write proper; to Victoria and Jeff for taking away my cowboy boots; to Pat for first getting me noticed outside; to Helen and Roni, Patsy, Valerie, and Joanne for keeping me sane (well, relatively); to Elaine for doing all the jobs I hate, always smiling, and being generally wonderful; to Paul, Ralphie, Lois, Diana, Daniella, Lori, Jerry, Maxine, Dave, Russ, Mark, and Gary for being there; to Bruce, Simon, and Jean-Philippe for teaching me the consulting profession; to Michael, Tim, and Martijn for protecting me when they didn't have to; to Larry, Tony, Roger, and the HPB crew for "the big picture"; to Jan, Serge, Maurice, Kenneth, and David for being pioneers in the Old World; to Kit, David, Chris, Darcio, Barry, Diana, Tonja, Julie, and Lisa for being pioneers in the New World; to Al C., Bob T., Tom C., and Pat McG. for their critiques; to Beth and Walter for their detailed reviews *and* sherried chicken in the Hollywood Hills; to Francis (close to an ADLer) for the best of the chapter headings and cartoon ideas, and other sparks of genius; to Glenda (honorary ADLer) for managing my '93 Tour; to Bret, Corinne, and Peter (increasingly honorary ADLers) for my '94 tour; to Dan and Ralph (almost ADLers) for Star Trek and the rest; to If (associate ADLer) for introducing me to system dynamics and lesser known malt whiskeys; to Patty O'Leary (who almost became an ADLer) for turning my complex descriptions into simple and beautiful cartoons; to Philip Ruppel (publisher to an ADLer) for wonderful insight and sensitivity to my writer's ego; to Fred Dahl (editor to an ADLer's publisher) for wonderful insight and sensitivty to my writing; to Al Wechsler for early interest; to Bob Curtice for building that interest in Caracas; to Scott Stricoff for then being interested enough to pioneer the study in Acorn Park; to Arun Maira for generous continuing support; to Ran Nayak for forcing rethink rather than incremental improvement; to Tom Sommerlatte for encouraging me in Europe; to Harland Riker for sponsoring me to the United States; to George Sacerdote for altruistically volunteering to give me a home; to to the wonderful Rulebuster core team: Celia Doremus for promoting me till even I wanted to learn more about unwritten rules; Jane Morris for pushing the marketing envelope to the limit and then trying to do more; to Debbie Adamian for untrained right-brain intuitive enthusiasm; to Todd Burger for an unbelievable job in getting a giant to run; and to Dave Shanks for inspirational enthusiasm and faith matched by hunger for results; to Tammy Erickson (my managing director, and, as far as I know, the highest-ranking female consultant in the world) for having the guts to back me to the hilt; and to Charlie LaMantia (one of those rare CEOs who consistently really does practice what he preaches) for creating an environment where all this was possible.

To each of you, and to all my other colleagues, clients, family, and friends who have contributed so much: Thank you.

Peter Scott-Morgan

The Unwritten Rules
of the Game

OK, Sam. That's fine. Now let's go for a <u>major</u> improvement in performance...

1
How to Fail in a Major Way

Shortcut to a Coronary

I remember the first time I sat down with the CEO of a global consumer products company. At that point he was two years into a major initiative to improve product development throughout his company—and the initiative was failing.

The recent history he gave on his company could have belonged to any of thousands of other firms. In the early 1980s, his chief competitors stepped up their performance. His company began losing market share and kept losing it for five consecutive years. He responded by downsizing and adopting total quality management, and in the late 1980s performance stabilized.

So he had a little breathing space. But he knew that he could not relax. He felt his responsibility was to keep pushing the company's performance to still higher levels. And the one area above all others that he was still not happy with was new product development. He wanted more exciting products and he wanted them faster. What's more, he knew that to achieve those sorts of improvements he would have to get all the different functions and divisions in the company to communicate and cooperate better than they ever had before.

The good news had been that when he began testing the water throughout the organization, people at all levels of the company agreed with him. In fact they started getting excited about it. So he encouraged their "bottom-up" enthusiasm with his own "top-down" support. He knew the importance of vision and leadership, so he put a lot of effort into providing them. In due course the high-profile improvement initiative was given a title: "Pulling Together into the Next Century." Everything seemed to be going well.

Two years later the initiative was deemed a complete failure.

When I met him, the CEO was looking chronically tired. For at least a year he had been rallying his troops as he watched enthusiasm die and cynicism take its place. At the back of his mind he must have begun worrying about the security of his own job. I recall that when he greeted me his lips drew into a smile but his eyes remained weary. And I remember that we talked for about an hour before he leaned back in his sofa and looked up at the ceiling and sighed.

"You know, Peter, we put tremendous effort into coming up with what we thought was a practical process for new product development.

We involved people, at the cutting edge, in teams ... all those good things. Then we had top managers 'walk the talk' so to speak. We had a cascade of training throughout the company.

"We measured everything. We did culture audits. We hired management gurus. We did it all by the book."

He sat forward. "And what we have now is 180 degrees opposite to what we set out to get. In fact, things are worse than before. Teamwork's poor. We have no cross-company cooperation, so our lead times are still abysmal. No one takes any creative risks, so our products are still unimaginative, even boring. On top of that, we have a new problem ... chronic short-termism."

He ended in utter frustration: "I don't understand what on earth I've done wrong!"

The tragedy was that he was well versed in management's best practice ... and he had applied it. He had known that what his company needed was teamwork, creativity, and longer term thinking ... and yet he had utterly failed to get them.

His experience is typical.

For the last eight years I have worked with the oldest and one of the largest international management consultancies, Arthur D. Little, Inc. The great luxury of working with any of the large consultancies is that you get a privileged insight to just what is going on in a wide range of businesses. You have a chance to see what trends are building within and across whole industries. And there is one massive trend that is growing in every industry and every country.

Failure.

And with failure—frustration. Every company I come in contact with has some type of major improvement initiative in progress. Senior executives spend increasingly sizable portions of their time shaping and guiding important change initiatives designed to improve performance in their businesses. Some aim to implement programs to increase business focus, to bring a complex set of customer, employee, and owner needs into balance, to speed up key business processes, or to streamline the resources and assets of their organizations. But most CEOs are disappointed with the results. They're finding that the quest for change is frustrating and the pace of change is slower than their organizations, or their personal careers, can stand.

As I write, we have just completed a detailed survey of 350 major companies across the United States. Almost every company turned out to be in the throws of a major change initiative—often to reduce overhead costs, streamline their organization or increase sales, typically driven by a change in leadership, change in business direction, financial, or competitive pressures. And over 80 percent of companies anticipated another major corporate change within the next few years.

Yet how satisfied were these companies with their current initiatives? Only 17 percent were really satisfied. Almost 40 percent were positively unsatisfied—often they had only gained partial success or else the whole initiative was taking too long. Nearly 70 percent of all the companies said they had experienced unanticipated problems and unintended side effects. Sixty-five percent said that their initiatives had been damaged by lack of buy in from managers and employees. And the next most common causes of damage? Turf battles, lack of a senior champion, and inadequate skills for managing change.

All these findings have been mirrored in other surveys conducted elsewhere. But the most disconcerting finding comes when you discuss the results with CEOs. Then you find that they're worried that they do not really understand what's going wrong. They conduct a post mortem, put the initiative on the table and nine times out of ten they find that it still looks sound on paper. The new strategy still makes sense. The process design still looks rigorous. But the hoped for benefits still do not fully materialize. So they continue to hit their heads against a brick wall. Or they give up and move onto the next approach that they hope will provide the quantum leap in performance that they're looking for. What is really sad is that people are becoming resigned to the inevitability of failure.

In fact, we are all growing to accept that whenever we attempt to implement a major change we are bound to hit hidden barriers. We are bound to fail to some extent. We have all experienced it. We are all learning to endure it. We tell ourselves: "That is the real world."

Well, maybe it's just me, but when you think about all this, doesn't it strike you as a bit bizarre? I mean, we can reliably access massive complexity in a book-sized computer, telephone via satellite straight to the other side of the world, safely fly tens of millions of people in and out of international airports, eradicate killer diseases such as tuberculosis, yet when it comes to implementing change within the neatly defined and relatively controllable confines of a business community none of us seems to know how to do it properly. And some people are starting to tacitly accept that fact as being inevitable.

And that's not good enough. It's not even necessary. By the end of this book you will understand why. In Part 1 you will see that the most damaging problems that organizations across the world are starting to face relate to the "soft" aspects of change—and you will probably recognize many of the problems from your own experience. In Part 2 you will learn how the unwritten rules of the game provide the missing link in understanding these aspects of failure. Not just what is going wrong, but *why* things are going wrong and, most importantly, *how* to track back to root causes and then do something about them.

In Part 3 you will learn the root causes of the nine most common barriers that damage business performance and an organization's ability to change. In Parts 4 and 5 you will understand how to track back to tangible management levers that will remove those barriers. Then in Part 6 you will study eight different examples of how a wide variety of organizations removed barriers found in their own businesses. In Part 7 you will examine five of the most insidious barriers to performance, and how to remove them. In Part 8 you will learn how to integrate mastery of the unwritten rules of the game into everyday management. At the end of the book there is a guide that details how you can uncover the unwritten rules within your own organization to provide guidance on removing barriers to change for specific improvement initiatives you have underway.

But enough of providing a reader's road map. First things first. What exactly is going on in the business community? What has led people throughout the world to feel that now as never before they need to understand how to remove "soft" barriers to change? Well, to start with, in the late 1980s an increasing number of organizations found that, despite all promises to the contrary, the classic approaches to total quality management (TQM) did not in reality result in total quality when applied to large, cross-functional processes such as product development or customer service. Indeed, some companies largely turned from TQM as a result. This created a vacancy at the top of the list of the "Ten Most Popular Management Ideas." Enter the next panacea: Business Process Reengineering ...

Bet the Company— and Lose

Business Process Reengineering is justifiably billed as one of the most important new approaches to performance improvement in this decade. It offers to address the next frontier of challenge: streamlining those complex activities of a business that straddle several departments. In the extreme you can start from a blank sheet of paper and rethink the underlying assumptions on which key aspects of your business operate. Then you can totally reengineer the old ways of doing things, often with massive potential improvements in productivity at all levels of the company.

Businesses worldwide are understandably excited at this prospect and are proving willing to commit substantial resources to reengineering. The sparks of their enthusiasm have been fanned by the more evangelical proponents of the new religion to the point where CEOs are routinely exhorted that they need to demonstrate their faith in radical reengineering by "being willing to bet the company."

Of course, it would help if reengineering actually worked.

The trouble is that even two of the leading gurus in the field, Mike Hammer and James Champy, admit that up to 70 percent of reengineering efforts fail to achieve results. Give or take a little bit, most experts these days privately agree that unless you are very clever about it, those are the chances of failure—mainly because people resist the change in one way or another. So, if you go so far as to bet your company, the current odds are—you'll lose.

Yet I frequently meet with CEOs who genuinely feel that they do not have a choice any more: If they do not manage to reengineer the company then in due course it will go under anyway. Most of these CEOs recognize that they need to do something practical to improve the company's chances of success, rather than bemoan the current success rate.

But a few succumb to *Macho Lemming Syndrome*.

Macho Lemming Syndrome

There is a certain type of male macho manager who loves the idea of rising to the challenge of betting the company when the established odds are at least seven to three against. For them there appears to be an intensely virile appeal to the idea, and you can almost smell the testosterone when you enter their office.

If they are even willing to discuss the idea that maybe, just maybe, they too will suffer from the "people problems" that so many others have faced, they will regale you with a speech on leadership. Although the details of the speech may vary, the main points inevitably are as follows.

"I think the key issue is *leadership*, don't you? The role of the manager is to develop a clear vision and then communicate it—clearly—to everyone. The reason that all these other people hit problems is because they don't take the time to explain to people what it is they're trying to do and why it makes sense.

"People have to have faith in your judgment. At the end of the day if something goes wrong—doesn't get implemented properly—it's the manager's fault. Isn't it? People shouldn't go whining about the people beneath them. They should get off their backsides and do their jobs!

"I really don't consider it … appropriate to waste too much time on the soft issues. Don't you agree? You've got to just get going and *lead!* It's that simple."

With that, like all the macho lemmings before them, they lead their employees over the edge of a cliff with the encouragement: "Don't be so weak! I see land ahead. Just swim to the other side."

Then they hit a hidden current flowing strongly against them. Unable to turn back, all the lemmings give everything they have to the uneven struggle, till eventually, exhausted, they sink in sight of land.

Jack the Ripper Hits New Wave

Of course, managers that get caught up in *Macho Lemming Syndrome* are not wrong when they lay such emphasis on leadership as the means to achieving substantial improvements in performance. It *is* vital—maybe above everything else. But during attempts at major change, like process reengineering, leadership alone has not proven sufficient to compensate for the hidden undercurrents of corporate culture and people's vested interests and private agendas.

It is crass to suggest that managers, like the consumer products CEO we met earlier, do not have sufficient vision or do not communicate that vision clearly enough to everyone in the body of their organizations. They do. Most managers these days are highly sophisticated. The leadership speech might have held true ten years ago, but it sounds dated and pompous today.

The reality is that we are all having to deal with a new set of problems that were only in their infancy a decade ago. Since the start of the 1980s there has been a new wave of management thinking: TQM, intrapreneuring, downsizing, management by walking around, empowerment, one minute managing, teamwork, reengineering, customer focus, learning organizations. The common denominator of all these new wave approaches is that to work they all require that we *change the ways people behave.*

That is fundamentally different to the type of management thinking of the 1970s and 1980s. Then we were deciding how to draw lines around distinct strategic business units or else focusing on which technologies could grant us the greatest competitive advantage. Apart from a few lone voices in sociotechnology and industrial sociology, behavior was the province of the Personnel department.

But about the same time that Personnel became Human Resources, the idea of new wave management started to take root. And one after another, each approach hit the same problem: Changing the ways people behaved was far more difficult than many had anticipated. Sustaining the change often proved impossible. Whether in the form of a quality drive or as part of Reorientating Toward the Customer, initiatives tended to have either a flare effect (in which everything seemed to move fast to start with, but then died down) or else were patchy and worked only in some parts of the business but not in others. Worse, nobody really felt that they knew what was going on.

It was at this point that, in many people's minds, behavioral barriers became the Jack the Ripper of corporate change. It had killed before and would kill again, but it was impossible to stop and impossible to track down. For managers who had been trained to have a neatly deterministic view of the corporate world, this was a strain to say the least.

Then, at the peak of the gung-ho, "greed-is-good-whatever-the-human-cost" 1980s, a disconcerting number of executives started to talk seriously about *corporate culture*. To many other people, what was particularly disconcerting about this was that most of the culprits did not have the excuse that they came from California. So even the most conservative traditionalist worried that maybe they should not dismiss the idea as a soft fad.

The concept of organizational culture was actually very new. The term had first been coined by the anthropologist Pettigrew in only 1979. In the short time since, culture and its relevance to business had shot to academic and professional respectability. Increasingly, the business press offered examples of good ideas that had become stuck in the cultural mire of "the way we do things here."

Yet by the end of the decade, more and more executives had come to recognize that invoking "corporate culture" as the barrier to change did not actually move things forward very much further. Locating the source of failure in the corporate culture might have sounded like a diagnosis, but it certainly did not lead to an effective cure.

As a result, companies tended to adopt one of four options. The first option was to accept with passive resignation the inevitably slow pace of change within their corporations. Sometimes they would wait large numbers of years before even trying to change—waiting for influential executives to retire and take with them the old company lore. But this approach is rarely feasible today. Most companies and most executives cannot afford to wait to grapple with change initiatives, many of which require dramatically different cultures from those now in place in order to succeed. John Akers lost his CEO job in large part because he could not deal fast enough with the strong tides of change that were pounding the immovable bulkhead of the IBM culture.

A second option companies adopted was to side step the embedded culture. Bring in some hired guns and tell them to "go out there and get it done!" But executing change around the backs of existing management proved a risky approach, expensive, and inevitably short-term.

The third option was to wait until the company was on the very brink of oblivion, on the theory that only when the organization's survival was at risk would people be willing to change their attitudes quickly. The trouble with this option was that by the time the organization was in such difficulties that everyone's minds were "concentrated wonderfully," the CEO found that the options available to the company had also been concentrated down wonderfully. Indeed, the viable options for survival were often so constrained that many managers found themselves wondering whether they really should have tried to do something earlier.

The fourth option was to call in self-styled experts in organizational culture and set out on what increasingly proved to be the long, disruptive, and costly task of trying to understand and change the corporate culture itself. Of all the options, to many CEOs this seemed like the most sensible approach: Change the culture to lay the groundwork for the other business changes to come. What none of us yet knew was why this task would turn out to be so all-encompassing and difficult.

Reincarnated after a century of slumber, the return of the Ripper was to prove a gratuitous horror story worthy of the sated palates of the late twentieth century. For now he was not stalking the back streets of Victorian London. Somehow the Ripper had got into the corridors of corporate power. And after each kill, the culture vultures swooped down ...

Flight of the Culture Vultures

Everybody had the best of intentions. The whole concept of corporate culture originated from the field of anthropology, and at the time none of us questioned whether or not that was a suitable foundation to start building from. During the 1980s everyone just leapt on the bandwagon. Academicians changed disciplines and joined consultants in the fray. More and more sophisticated models were devised, but in essence the approach remained the same as anthropologists had used a century earlier to analyze the culture of new tribes that they discovered up the Amazon.

In other words the models *described* culture. Some models distinguished group norms from organizational values, some looked for rituals and artifacts, some differentiated culture from climate, but in essence they just noted what was there. And the same is true to this day. Although there are some sophisticated models that claim to show the links between such concepts as climate and motivation, or leadership and management practices, they are still in essence descriptive models, merely showing the potential influence of one concept on another.

I remember in the mid 1980s getting really excited by culture audits and climate indexes. But the trouble was that after you had conducted such an audit, and described (sometimes in excruciating detail) just what was there, you tended to find that you were not very much further. You might gather unimpeachable evidence that teamwork was a problem, or that innovation was not highly regarded. But then what did you do? The models tended to provide little or no guidance on how to proceed any further—how actually to improve the situation. So how did people respond? They resorted to trying to teach teamwork, encourage a quality attitude, and train company values. What a waste of time that turned out to be.

I was sharing a conference platform recently with one of the world authorities on quality. Off the record he told me that over the last few years he had been working with certain companies that had probably put more effort into trying to teach new values than any other corporations in the world. And he said that in his heart he did not believe that they had made the slightest difference.

14

That is an increasingly common refrain from top executives as well. More and more confess to me that they feel they have had their fingers burnt by those they now describe as "culture vultures." They claim that they got results that although interesting were often no surprise. And they complain that the same studies gave rise to implementation plans that were too soft and fuzzy to be of any use. They claim they are now doubly cynical about addressing cultural issues in the future. After all, they started off not really believing you could tackle the issues in a pragmatic way, and they feel that that has been borne out.

Yet all this is not really fair to the anthropologists. After all, the purpose of academic anthropology has been to describe and measure culture, typically as a baseline for preserving it—never with the intent to change it. As a result, the models that we all took from anthropology and then modified *were never intended to act as blueprints for change*. And big surprise: They have not delivered the goods.

Why? Because deep down there is no cause and effect built into the models. When we apply those models to corporations as a means of accelerating change we are stumbling around in the dark ages of change management. It is no more advanced than alchemy.

In the dark ages of chemistry, you would start burning some wood bark, throw some sulfur and saltpeter into a bowl, walk in a circle counterclockwise 13 times, chanting and bowing to the moon, then throw in the ashes from the bark. And if you did everything exactly as specified you got a magical substance that now we call gunpowder.

But if you missed anything out of the ritual then you often got nothing but an inert black powder; so you had to do everything by rote. Yet if only you had understood the link of cause and effect you would have known that the walking and the chanting and the bowing were necessary not because of the walking, chanting, and bowing themselves, but because of the time that they took so that the wood bark could fully carbonize.

The anthropologically-based models for conducting culture audits suffer from the same handicap. They are derived from academic models that were never intended to do more than describe—so never needed to build in cause and effect. As a result, the so-called culture audits that we all got so excited about were not even real audits at all because they provided no mechanism to verify what was actually going on.

It's as if we went into a company and took a photocopy of the balance sheet and the profit and loss account, noted the color of the leather binding on a ledger, recorded the pattern on the carpet in the Accounts department, and wrote a memo documenting the age, make, color, and weight of one of the doors of the car driven by the chief financial officer and claimed that we had just conducted a financial audit. Of course we haven't. All we have done is record a large number of facts all loosely related to finance. Do they all have links to finance? Yes, but just as when we conduct a culture audit we have no idea when to stop, where to draw the line. Should we expect all these facts to guide us in improving the process of financial bookkeeping? No. Should we expect them to serve any practical purpose at all—other than act as an interesting record of what the finance department is like? Probably not.

At the end of the day, no one within an organization has ever had to consult a detailed audit of shared values and beliefs, artifacts, role models, myths, and rituals and the interrelationships between them before they could decide how to act. And yet large groups of people within a company nevertheless all manage to act in similar ways—hence the concept of corporate culture in the first place.

So maybe we were all being too clever in coming up with academic constructs that did not correspond to the ways people actually interpreted their environments—the ways *we* interpret *our* environment. Maybe ten years ago we should have come down from the clouds and looked inside ourselves to think what was actually driving our own behavior, rather than come up with grandiose constructs relating to culture.

If only we had, we would have found that there was indeed a more pragmatic, leaner way to come to grips with behavioral barriers to effective change. We would have understood that most of the time, charting corporate culture is not even necessary. What is more, we would have realized that we knew the key insight all along. It is the secret that everyone already knows.

?

Of course I don't want to learn about market research, Adams!
I'll be promoted to <u>another</u> totally new job in six months ...

2
The Secret
Everyone Knows

Rule of the Rules

Forget everything you've ever been taught. Look inside yourself. What is the honest advice that you would give a friend about how to get on in your organization? In reality, how do you need to behave and why? Who is actually important, and why? In general, what do people in the organization really want out of their work, and what do they want to avoid? Given that, what are the sensible ways to act, things to do, people to deal with? In practice, what would get you sidelined or fired? Who is it that you do not really need to worry about? What must you always do? What are the rules of the game that your friend should follow ... that you follow?

Now move out of the work environment. Ask yourself the equivalent questions about your favorite social activity. Ask the questions about your extended family. Ask them about the country you live in. Ask them about driving in your local city.

Did you need to be told the answers by an expert? Of course not. Were the answers reasonably obvious? Probably—particularly when you were thinking about situations and environments that were close to your daily personal experience. Did you find that you knew some of the answers even though you had never consciously thought through them before? Again, probably yes. You do not need to have explicitly formulated rules of the game to know what they are and how to act accordingly.

In every realm of our lives there are rules of the game. Whether we're at work or play, with family or colleagues, friends or strangers, we all act according to an often unspoken set of rules. And if you think about it a bit further, you will realize that the rules always seem to come in two forms: the written rules and the unwritten rules.

As an illustration, imagine driving in any of the various cities that are famous for their homicidal taxi drivers. I live in both Europe and the United States, so my closest examples are Boston and Paris. In both cities, the drivers' manual says that when you get to a main road you are supposed to slow down, wait your turn, and merge courteously with the flow of traffic.

I tried that. You find that no one lets you onto the main road. The drivers behind you tolerate this for about five seconds. Then they start to blow their horns, wind their windows down, and gesticulate.

The unwritten rules of the road in Boston and Paris say that when approaching a main road avoid eye contact, speed up, and do not wait your turn, because it is nobody's turn. Then you try to shoot ahead of the cars already on the main road before they can get you. If you want to be pragmatic, and get onto that main road, you need to understand the unwritten rules.

Corporations also have unwritten rules. If you're behind the wheel of the corporation, it pays to understand the unwritten rules. Knowing the rules of the game is another way to be street smart about your business. In fact, I've never met a top manager who had managed to get to the top without having an intuitive grasp of the unwritten rules of their organization. The unwritten rules are what help people survive and thrive. They are highly sensible coping skills for all employees—not just those destined for the top.

But where do the unwritten rules in companies actually come from? They typically start with top management. On the one hand the unwritten rules come from the way top managers behave—their actions and their pronouncements—and on the other hand with what you can think of as the written rules that they create or maintain.

By the way, throughout this book I will use a very wide definition of written rules. The term is meant to cover all the formal, official, and understood aspects of the business. It includes everything from the very broad aspects of vision statements, organization structure and policies, to the more specific aspects of strategy, procedures, process descriptions, and reward systems.

All the various written rules, together with the behavior and actions of top management, send signals into the body of an organization. But then various factors go to work on the signals—factors that no managers can control or even measure: things like national and local culture, the economic climate, legislation, regulation, people's private agendas, and existing unwritten rules.

All these factors transform the signals being sent into the organization—reinforcing them, undermining them, twisting them—until the original management actions and written rules have a complete set of parallel unwritten rules that actually drive people's day-to-day behavior. An important insight is that all the factors that transform the original signals are for practical purposes beyond anyone's immediate control. You may need to anticipate them and compensate for them, but you're unlikely able to change them.

That can be a real problem. Maybe you're a CEO and you set up a formal open door policy and you reinforce it at every opportunity by telling your managers, "I really want your ideas and suggestions." But given people's private agendas, it's so easy for that to turn into an unwritten rule: "Use the open door to get visibility with the CEO ... but only tell her what she wants to hear." And if the CEO ever once makes the mistake of shooting the messenger when someone brings bad news, then naturally that unwritten rule will be reinforced still further. Employees will rationalize that the safest way to keep in favor and keep the CEO informed is for them to be, shall we say, economical with the truth.

The sequence is typical of the ways we pick up the unwritten rules. It's the advice we get from a knowing friend, or the guidance we're given when we first join the company and then either have borne out by experience or else disregarded as being the "official version." It's the signals we pick up as to what we really have to do to get on in our organizations. And maybe the most powerful signals of all come from when we see someone sidelined or fired.

The unwritten rules of the game correspond to the internal politics of a business—even when nobody within the organization would complain that their colleagues were political. The point is that, when it matters to us, we are *all* politically correct. The unwritten rules reflect enlightened self interest.

And their existence, of course, is as old as mankind. So the importance of the unwritten rules of the game is not in recognizing their existence. It is not in giving them a name. They have, after all, been recognized and named many times before: politics, social norms, tacit understanding.

Their importance to the pragmatic manager is that they provide the key insight needed to really get things to happen in an organization. And that insight only becomes apparent when you burrow one level deeper than the unwritten rules of the game themselves, and examine how the unwritten rules develop and interact in the business world ...

The Good, the Bad, and the Ugly

Every organization has unwritten rules of the game. Indeed, every organization is a creature of its unwritten rules. But unwritten rules are not good or bad. They are just appropriate or inappropriate given what the organization is trying to achieve. And the real problems occur when unwritten rules reinforce each other in ways that no one recognizes.

Remember the CEO of the consumer products company whose product development initiative had failed? Let me describe the internal environment in which he introduced his new initiative. As an example of how the unwritten rules develop from written rules, I'll give just three of the company's top-level policies.

The first written rule said: "To become a top manager, you must be well-rounded. You need breadth of experience across the company." At the start of his change initiative, the CEO registered that this formal policy was ideal because it would encourage exactly the sort of cross-business perspective that was needed for the new product development initiative to work.

The second written rule was targeted at the top 10 percent of managers—the high flyers. It said: "The best performing managers get accelerated promotion from their boss." In practice, high flyers tended to move up every two years. Again, this was seen as highly complementary to the new initiative because the best managers would see the potential benefits of striving to make the initiative work.

The third written rule was typical of many companies. It said: "The chief performance measure for managers is the profit and loss of their area." This too was seen to be conducive with the new initiative, because everyone would feel accountable.

Now you can begin to see why, with such a platform, the CEO was confident he could make the product development initiative a tremendous success. Unfortunately, the information that I've just given is all we need to know that the whole improvement initiative was actually doomed to failure from the start.

To understand why, you need to look at the unwritten rules within the body of the company. Soon after my initial meeting with the CEO, my colleagues and I applied a methodology that I devised in the 1980s to uncover and codify unwritten rules of the game. It's the same methodology that's explained in the guide at the end of this book. Here's what we found.

Where the written rule said: "To become a top manager, you need broad experience," the unwritten rule said: "To get to the top, job-hop as fast as possible." People recognized that they had to get through ten grades in as many years if they were to have a chance for the top. And if that was what it took, then that was what they were going to do.

Where the second written rule said: "The best performing managers get accelerated promotion from their boss," we found at least three strongly related unwritten rules. First, "Keep your boss happy." After all, he or she is the one handing out the transfers and promotions. Second, "Stand out from the crowd"—so you'll be noticed as a top performer. Finally, "Avoid association with failure; never let your boss see you fail."

Where the third written rule said: "Managers are accountable for their profit and loss," we found another two unwritten rules: "Protect your own turf," and "Watch your quarterlies."

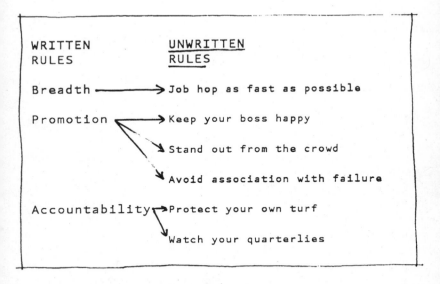

Now consider the impact of all those unwritten rules taken together. With rules like "Stand out from the crowd," and "Protect your own turf," it's easy to see why teamwork just was not working. Combine that with keeping a boss, who wants to protect his or her own turf, happy and you'll not risk appearing disloyal by apparently "wasting" time working with other parts of the business.

The chronic short-termism encouraged by job-hopping and the focus on quarterly results was not new as the CEO had believed. It was only newly apparent—exposed by the new emphasis on longer term thinking and teamwork needed for successful product development. And who's going to take a personal risk in an organization like this, when so much depends on continuing short-term success to keep climbing the corporate ladder?

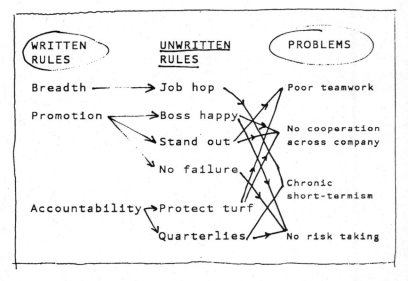

So what's going on here? How did we move from apparently highly positive written rules to such damaging behavior? Is this typical or is it a special case? I've now used the unwritten rules of the game approach in large numbers of corporations in the United States, Europe, Latin America, and the Far East. My colleagues are applying the technique worldwide. We all keep finding similar hidden conflicts to those of the consumer products company. The details are different, and the unwritten rules of some companies are certainly very different indeed. But in every case, unwritten rules derived from apparently innocuous written rules or management behavior, nevertheless create major conflicts with new change initiatives.

But consider the analysis of the consumer products company. The conflicts were only explained by looking at the unwritten rules. It was only when we understood "The way things really work around the company" that it all started to make some sort of sense. The unwritten rules are the *missing link in our understanding*.

What's more, once we understand the unwritten rules, we see that what the CEO originally thought of as problems, were actually unintended negative side effects caused by hidden inconsistencies between the existing written rules or management behavior and his new change initiative. And the way in which apparently innocuous written rules and management behavior can create these hidden inconsistencies turns out to be typical.

One of the very important lessons that we've learned over the last few years is that the unintended negative side effects that undermine companies' best efforts usually *come from* apparently unconnected written rules or management behaviors. That's why they are not obvious. That's why even the best senior executives do not spot the link of cause and effect.

Think about it: If you cannot codify the unwritten rules within the body of your company and understand their implications, you can *never* predict where Jack the Ripper is going to spring from to kill your next change program.

It's not just listing the unwritten rules themselves that's so important—most people within a company feel they could probably list most of their organization's rules quite easily—what is vital is the ability to uncover the *links* between the unwritten rules and the unintended side effects that are showing themselves as business problems. And just as vital is finding the links between the offending unwritten rules and the *written* rules and management behaviors that are actually driving them but which may otherwise appear unrelated to the business problems.

The secret that everyone knows, but which few have thought through, is not the existence of the unwritten rules; it is not even the detail of what those rules happen to be. The real secret is that there is a chain of logical cause and effect that can be traced from specific business problems *via the unwritten rules* all the way back to the written rules and management actions that drive the company. And that means you can do something about them.

Decoding Success as Well as Failure

There is another very important lesson that we've learned over the last few years, and it's far more upbeat. It's that unwritten rules do not always thwart senior management. Quite the contrary—unintended side-effects are sometimes very positive. They remain unintended and unexplained, but at least they are acting as catalysts rather than barriers to change.

There is a major financial institution in the United States that's very pleased with the work of its special private banking division aimed at rich celebrity customers. Without many written rules or much training, the private banking employees have developed a highly effective system. Not only is top management pleased with its private bankers, but its clients are very happy as well. The trouble is, the CEO wants to spread this wonderful unwritten culture to another part of the bank, only he's not sure how to do it. What he now realizes is that he needs to know which of the bank's unwritten rules provide a competitive advantage.

Mastering the unwritten rules is more than just a method of remedying failure; it is also a method of replicating success. In other words, uncovering the unwritten rules of the game will not just help a company understand the hidden sources of failure in one part of its business, but can also help the company understand the hidden sources of success in another part of the business.

The same philosophy is true of *benchmarking*. Many companies are finding that they cannot just mimic *excellent* companies or *best practice* from other firms. They need to understand why it works in those companies and whether it might work in their own. "Fit" is all-important, but you can only understand the degree of fit by exploring the unwritten rules.

Of course, that raises the interesting question of how you actually uncover the unwritten rules in the first place.

The Needle, the Haystack, and the Magnet

Ever since the 1980s, when I developed the first methodologies for uncovering and changing the unwritten rules of the game, I suppose the most common question that people have asked me is: "OK, so what's the secret? How can we do something about the unwritten rules of our company?" The secret is actually relatively simple and is explained fully in the remainder of this book. In essence, it's a technique to uncover, codify, and change the unwritten rules systematically but to do so in a way that focuses *only on the rules that are affecting specific business issues.*

You can concentrate your efforts. Maybe you want to improve customer service or sales productivity, or reduce leadtimes or bureaucracy, or encourage cross-functional cooperation. Or maybe you have to implement a major change such as a reengineered process and perhaps your managers don't want to support it because they feel threatened. Whatever it is that you're trying to do, you only need to uncover the unwritten rules that are relevant to what you are aiming for. Although uncovering all of the unwritten rules in an organization may be of academic interest, I have yet to hit a situation where it would be of any practical benefit. It's far better to focus.

The first step is to start with the business issues that are giving people in your company ulcers. The original issue that the CEO of the consumer products company was concerned about was improving his product development process. That's your starting point. You begin by listening to a carefully selected group of people, encouraging them to talk generally all around this topic. And as they talk, they tell you the unwritten rules and how they are creating barriers to business performance and there you have it.

Well, alright. It isn't quite so simple. Uncovering the unwritten rules like that would be like hunting for a needle in a haystack. There are so many comments that would get in the way that you would almost certainly miss what was most important. What you need is a magnet to locate the needle. What you get are actually three magnets that help you separate out all the important aspects of what people tell you.

Now, *concentrate*. Don't skim the next few pages. The concepts explained in the next paragraphs will haunt you throughout the rest of the book. They are key to understanding the unwritten rules.

The first magnet is *motivators*. It corresponds to what is important to the people you are talking with. What motivates them? What makes them get up in the morning? What do they perceive as a reward? Just as important, what do they want to avoid? What do they perceive as a penalty?

In other words, you cluster together a list of the real carrots and sticks that the interviewees respond to. Not what they're supposed to be, but what they actually are: for example, exciting work, money, career advancement, respect, or (very common after a downsizing) being allowed to keep your job so you can continue paying the mortgage.

In the consumer products company, we found that one of the most important motivators for people was career advancement. They tended to be very ambitious and wanted to climb to the top of the company, and that became very clear in our early interviews. What's more, you'll remember, everyone knew that to climb to the top they needed breadth of experience. So there's a direct link between the unwritten rule "Job hop as fast as possible" and the motivator "Career advancement."

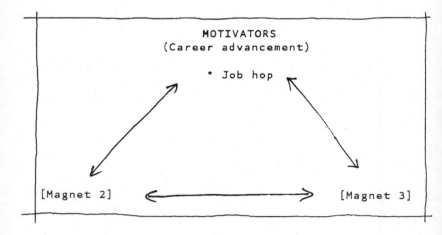

But, of course, closely associated with *what* is important to our interviewees is *who* is important. Who are the people that can enable the interviewees to get what's important to them? This second magnet is called *enablers*. It corresponds to the people who can grant the rewards or impose the penalties that are clustered under motivators. This heading really encapsulates the power structure of the company, as perceived by those within it. It's what a company president recently told me he called *the unwritten organization.*

In the consumer products company example, one of the key enablers was the line boss who could accelerate the promotion of real high flyers. Now, even before our interviewee tells us any unwritten rules, we can almost predict what they ought to be: "Keep your boss happy," "Stand out from the crowd," "Avoid association with failure." And you'll remember that those are exactly what we did find. They're the sensible ways to behave given people's interpretations of who's important. Indeed, if subsequently we find that there are different unwritten rules than those predicted, then it means that we do not fully understand the enablers. There has to be logical consistency.

That is also, by the way, the reason why you can use the same approach even when the most important rules are not only unwritten but also unspoken. Even in the most political of organizations, the test of logical coherence lets you unravel the truth. I have never found anyone who could lie consistently for up to two hours at the level of detail verified by the framework.

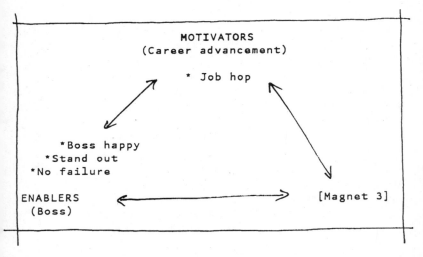

The third and final magnet, *triggers,* links the previous two. The triggers are the conditions people perceive need to be satisfied to get promoted. Here we put the triggers that cause the boss to grant that accelerated promotion. They correspond to the perceived performance measures.

In our case study, the key performance measure is a manager's bottom line—profit and loss. That's where we look for another set of unwritten rules. And sure enough, you'll remember they are as logical, and as predictable for us to look out for in the interviews, as all the others. "Protect your own turf," and "Watch your quarterlies."

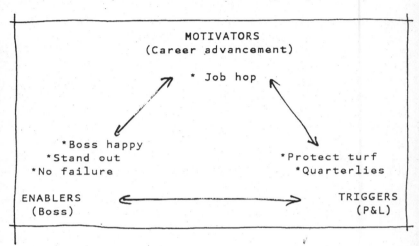

What we're really doing is focusing on *what* is important to people, and given what is important then *who* is important to them and *how* do they go about getting it. What ... Who ... How.

Using that approach, my colleagues at Arthur D. Little and I have found that large groups within a company all recognizably share the same rules. Contrary to what many would claim, large samples are not necessary. You do not need to disrupt your organization with vast numbers of interviews and questionnaires. You can often uncover the key unwritten rules relating to a specific business issue by talking with about only a dozen people within your organization. And that's a vital short cut, because having uncovered the unwritten rules, as we saw earlier, it becomes easy to understand why they inevitably result in the unintended side effects.

Now we've built up a long chain of cause and effect. The previously unexplained problems are actually seen to be unintended side effects. These side effects are caused by people acting according to unwritten rules, which are themselves sensible ways to act given people's perceptions of what and who is important and how you go about getting it— the motivators, enablers, and triggers.

We're almost done. We have almost traced back from the apparently soft behavioral problems all the way to something that we can actually do something about. The final link of the chain is to tie the motivators, enablers, and triggers back to the written rules or management actions that are inconsistent with our change initiative and are causing all the problems. If only we can do that, then we will at last be able to make the realignments necessary to eradicate the problems.

The icing on the cake is that we're already there. The motivators, enablers, and triggers *already correspond* to people's perceptions of the net effect of all the company's written rules and management actions.

Motivators relate to policies and top-management behavior such as remuneration, job content, career progression, status, training, hiring, and firing. In other words, they relate to specific types of actions, policies, and procedures—specific types of "management levers."

Enablers relate to job descriptions, organization charts, reporting lines, and sign-off responsibilities. Again, specific things that you can actually do something about.

Triggers relate to such things as performance measures, milestone descriptions, evaluation charts, objectives, and strategy. Again, tangible things. Finally, we can determine what drives the behavioral barriers to performance.

The supreme tragedy of the consumer products company example is one of timing. For, in reality, the CEO could have conducted the unwritten rules of the game analysis two years previously. He could have used the analysis to *predict* the unintended negative side effects two years earlier than he actually did. As a result, he could have saved his company, and himself, two years of unnecessary torture.

Smoke and Mirrors

Viewing organizations from the perspective of the unwritten rules of the game reminds me of the optics experiments at school. Remember what they were like? You would shine a set of beams into an optics box that had mirrors or a prism inside it. Then you would observe the resultant image that was projected out the other side onto a screen.

Well, the beams are your written rules. They go into the black box of "corporate culture" and get influenced by a whole host of factors, most of which you do not even know about. But you see the results, in the form of your corporate performance—your "screen" of the organization.

Now you bring in a change initiative—a new light source that you shine into the black box from a new direction. Suddenly there are all sorts of interference patterns on the screen. Some things are reinforced and some things disappear, and you don't know what's going on.

So what do you do? You blow smoke onto the optics bench so that you can see the beams of light. That's like uncovering the unwritten rules. We're not so much interested in the unwritten rules themselves so much as what they tell us about what's going on. As the beams go through the prism—even though we cannot observe it directly— they indicate what is happening within the black box of culture. The prism corresponds to the interlinked trio of motivators, enablers, and triggers.

And, as in the optics experiment, once we understood what was going on, we could realign the light sources to minimize interference—so, in the same way, we can realign the written rules or management actions with our change initiative. We will look at just how to do the realignment in Parts 5, 6, and 7 of this book.

Managing Through Empathy

Some managers believe that they can compensate for the unwritten rules through intuition. In the past, the best managers could. Indeed, I said before that every top manager has an intuitive grasp of the unwritten rules. So why is that not enough any more?

It's because intuition is based on experience, and experience is of the past. And at times of rapid change or major change (such as downsizing or process reengineering or shifts in the economy) intuition from the past frequently doesn't hold any more. In fact, the unintended side effects caused may even become counterintuitive. Increasingly, top managers are conceding to me that they feel they are "losing it." They're starting to feel isolated and out of touch. They cannot accurately predict how their organizations will respond any more.

The problem is still greater when an executive joins a company at the top. I pose these questions to any new CEO joining a company: "Coming from outside the corporation, will your new regime appreciate the unwritten rules and act accordingly? Will you understand what hidden benefits come from the existing policies and procedures, even the apparent bureaucracy, so that you can make major changes without 'throwing the baby out with the bath water?' Or will you write new written rules and act in ways that wind up creating unintended negative side effects that create even more problems, more hidden risks, and more damage?"

It will be no surprise to you by now, that my advice to *all* managers is: Ensure that you understand the full implications of the unwritten rules in the body of your organization. These days, to be a true leader you need far greater empathy, insight, and rigor than is possible informally. You need new tools to cope with a new reality. You also need to learn to view the world through other people's eyes. So, let's have a peek.

So, <u>what</u> was it you wanted to tell me about your latest sales projections?

3
The Voyeurs' Guide to the Real World

Nine Windows
onto Reality

Mastering the unwritten rules of the game is the way to become a modern day troubleshooter. You can react to or predict barriers to performance, rapidly track down the real causes, and correct them. And like any troubleshooter, you build on experience and recognize patterns.

Indeed, one of the greatest joys I've found of being an unwritten rules troubleshooter is that you get invited to become a voyeur of so many different organizations. Within a very short time you're peeling back layers of facade, picking up all the best gossip, understanding what really makes the organization tick, and comparing and contrasting what you find with all the other organizations you've been invited into. Even better, that's exactly what you're there to do. It's wonderful.

After many years of such voyeurism, I began to recognize some recurring themes. The patterns corresponded to types of unintended negative side effects caused by conflicts between new change initiatives and existing motivators, enablers, and triggers.

As we proceed, I'll be running through nine descriptions of the most common types of side effects found within corporations of all sizes and across all industries. Of course, there are many other kinds of side effects, but these are the most common. Likewise, there are infinite variations in the detail of each type of side effect, but the broad pattern remains consistent.

The nine side effects that follow are not just a random list. Three correspond to side effects that are set up when a new change is introduced that is in strong conflict with existing motivators. Three correspond to conflicts with enablers, and the final three to conflicts with triggers.

In practice, there are other side effects in organizations that, when you analyze them, you find are driven by strong conflicts with both motivators and enablers, enablers and triggers, triggers and motivators, or sometimes with all three. Although this is quite common, the resultant side effects are themselves usually combinations of the nine most common side effects.

If a new change initiative is in conflict with existing	MOTIVATORS	ENABLERS	TRIGGERS
THEN YOU GET: ⟶	3 common side effects	Another 3 common side effects	Yet another 3 common side effects

Each triad of side effects (corresponding respectively to motivators, enablers, and triggers) also follows a structure. The first side effect corresponds to pressure from the new change initiative that feels weaker to people in the organization than the conflicting pressure from the existing unwritten rules. The second side effect corresponds to when people feel a near balance between the pressure from the new initiative and the old rules. The third side effect occurs when the pressure from the new initiative feels stronger than the pressure from the conflicting unwritten rules.

In reality, the triads of side effects are just three points on a spectrum. When a new change initiative is introduced (usually unintentionally) in head-on conflict with existing and important unwritten rules, the generic type of side effect created seems very dependent on how strongly the new initiative is being enforced. This is true for conflicts with motivators, enablers, as well as triggers.

Broadly, if the pressure from a new initiative feels very weak, then the typical reaction is one of indifference, with people making hardly any changes in behavior to accommodate the new motivator, enabler, or trigger. If the initiative had not been in conflict with existing rules of the game, or if the conflicting unwritten rules were not perceived as very important, then the change would probably nevertheless have been accepted, but because it doesn't fit, it gets lost. This is such an obvious side effect that it's not included in the following list. Instead, the three points on the spectrum relate to when the conflicting pressure from the new initiative feels so strong that you can no longer ignore it.

The interesting question then becomes: Is the way to break through the conflict simply to push the new initiative harder, as many managers instinctively do when they hit resistance? Should they follow an equivalent approach to the way the English used to be taught to speak in a foreign country? Namely, if the natives don't understand you the first time—repeat the same words in English, but slower and *louder*.

What you find is that as the pressure from a new initiative increases, so the broad kind of side effect caused by its inherent conflict with existing important unwritten rules shifts from passive indifference, to increasingly active resistance, to struggle and conflict. Far from breaking through the resistance, the harder you push the conflicting new initiative, the greater the resistance to its implementation.

Yet most interesting of all, if you push still harder, if you really try to ram the new initiative home ... *the resistance goes undercover*. It does not disappear at all, although it seems to. The old unwritten rules do not realign with the new initiative, although they may appear to. The new initiative does not get implemented in a sustainable way, even though the risks for the future are often all too well hidden.

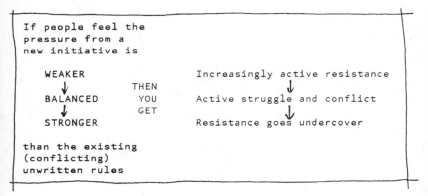

The undercover side effects (caused by pushing an initiative that's in strong conflict with existing unwritten rules) are the most dangerous and damaging of all side effects. Like a corporate cancer, they remain undetected for years, until the symptoms they cause become so severe that they cannot be masked any more. But by then it's often too late to guarantee a successful cure. As with cancer, the best strategy for long-term survival is early diagnosis—not ignoring the problem.

Enough of talking in generalities. Let's get down to details.

From Rebellion to Anarchy

In 1801, Horatio Nelson was second in command of a British fleet preparing to attack Copenhagen. Soon they came under heavy fire from shore guns, so pragmatic Admiral Parker, commander-in-chief of the British, arranged for a set of flags to be run up signalling the order to stop fighting. Aboard his own ship, Nelson was alerted to the signal. However, convinced he could see a way to win the attack, he raised his telescope to the eye he had lost in battle several years earlier: "I can't see any such signal," he replied to his deputy. "We'll continue to fight." They did, the British won, and Nelson was made a viscount. People have been "turning a blind eye" to the signals sent by their bosses ever since.

When a weak signal is sent that conflicts with existing triggers (the conditions that need to be satisfied to get what you want) then the most natural response is a form of *corporate rebellion*. You can't completely ignore the signal, but it feels weak enough that you can take the attitude "This too will pass," and so you can deliberately disregard it.

The XYZ Form gets introduced; but people can't see how it relates to them, so few bother to fill it out. A memo advises that managers should spend at least a week a year on an accredited training program in order to get their next grade; but everyone knows that you don't really need to go. Project milestones are signed off even when they're not fully completed. Some pay is linked to corporate performance but more is tied to individual success, so very few feel a high personal priority to work toward corporate as opposed to local performance improvement.

If there are many weak triggers in an organization then everyone starts to disregard everything. What was rebellion, when related to a few isolated examples, then turns into *corporate anarchy*. Bad move.

From Camouflage to Gridlock

Balance sounds like such a positive attribute. The trouble is that when applied to conflicting triggers (or indeed enablers or motivators) it's equivalent to Newton's Third Law: "For every action there's an equal and opposite reaction." When a conflicting trigger is strongly imposed, people can no longer get away with turning a blind eye. So what do they do? They start to play games: *corporate camouflage.* Accounts departments tend to be expert. Some of the creativity that goes into such mundane budget items as Other, Training, or Consultancy is worthy of an Oscar nomination. And that's nothing compared to what has to be accomplished around the year end.

But it's not just Accounts. To be honest, I've never come across any department that was not expert. I remember one factory manager who explained that he was measured on keeping inventory down. So once a month a convoy of trucks arrived, emptied the warehouse, drove around while the factory was audited, and then brought everything back.

Elsewhere, leadtimes are finessed by changing the definition of the start time; performance measures and benchmarks are selected so that they'll provide easy wins; market share is defined in terms of carefully specified customer groups. The list is fascinating and endless.

But as with weaker triggers, the nature of the side effect changes depending on whether the conflict creating it is a special case or is just one of many similar examples. When there is a large number of balanced conflicting triggers, everyone is playing games. No one can understand what is truly going on. Massively complex bureaucracies sometimes develop to compensate with red tape. More and more conflicting triggers are introduced and very soon it's not even theoretically possible to introduce a new trigger without it conflicting with many of the triggers already in place. At this stage an organization moves toward *corporate gridlock.* Some of the government organizations I've come across are well on their way already.

From Paranoia to Panic

Sometimes an inherently conflicting trigger, for instance a new performance measure, is forced through in such a way that the pressure to conform with the new measure feels even stronger than the counter-pressure from the existing triggers. In effect, what's happening is that the new trigger is signalling: "Do this if you want to get what you perceive as a reward or avoid what you perceive as a penalty," while the existing triggers continue to signal: "Do the exact opposite."

A common example in financial institutions is where there is a strong new message from the top: "We all need to be more creative and stop playing safe all the time"—for instance on financial lending. But this is often introduced against the backdrop of a very clear trigger: "In this institution, if you make a mistake you are punished"— often by the ruining of your career. The natural reaction? No one can go around discrediting the new trigger; indeed many intellectually agree with it but cannot whole heartedly follow it. Like laboratory rats that get electric shocks no matter what they do, such employees cannot win. This leads to *corporate paranoia*. People hide behind committee structures or else ensure that absolutely everything is documented so they can cover their backs. Productivity suffers and the organization begins to show stress.

It's remarkably easy for it to begin. A top executive of one of the most successful banks in the United States—which pushes customer service as its prime goal—explained to me recently that even they had manufactured a minor version of corporate paranoia. Tellers were only allowed two errors in the books before they were fired. Result: long customer queues as tellers tried to provide efficient service yet remain methodical.

But sometimes after heavy downsizing, or acquisition, or changes of top management, there are too many examples of strong conflicting triggers; paranoia turns to *corporate panic*. Like deer caught in head-lights, employees do not know which way to turn. The whole organization freezes. Under these conditions the unwritten rules can kill.

From Isolation to Impotence

We have all met the individual who has been appointed to an impressive sounding role but has "all responsibility and no authority." Some of us have been that individual. It can be a thankless task. It's a near impossible task if what you have to do runs counter to what the unwritten rules dictate that everyone else wants to achieve.

Such is the destiny of a new enabler—someone who supposedly can provide what's important to people—if he or she cannot actually provide what's important to people. Under these circumstances the pressure the new enabler is able to exert on people is likely to be far inferior to that exerted by the established unwritten rules. Remember, although enablers are often individuals, they can also be groups of people such as an "old boy's network," or even technology such as a computer system. A new enabler may compete with any or all of these.

The unintended side effect that arises from a weak new enabler in conflict with existing rules is different from what we found with triggers. Here the natural reaction is *corporate isolation*. The new enabler is simply bypassed or disregarded. Frequently, the only recourse for such an enbler is to become a blocker rather than a facilitator—a very negative role. It's the classic problem of many head office staff functions. The same side effect occurs when new technology, be it voice mail or desktop computing, is introduced but not tied into how people work.

Just as with triggers, the nature of the side effect changes if the conflicting weak enabler is more than just a special case. If too many people do not have any real power, because they're not integral to important motivator-enabler-trigger relationships, then the whole organization becomes sluggish. Everyone is worrying about pleasing their boss's boss or keeping their network happy. This leads to *corporate impotence* with the classic symptom: "There's not really any one person who can make that decision." Heaven alone can help if that sort of organization needs to respond quickly to changes in the industry.

From Power Play to Civil War

"Production can't make what R&D developed; now Sales say that they want something different anyway," or "It's just a turf battle," or "I don't care what she said, *I* want it done this way," or "Did nobody think to ask me?" or "You're out of your jurisdiction," or "Just don't push it!" We all have our stories of the battles that rage between one department and another, between one individual and another, between fresh blood and the old guard. We even call them war stories. They're the classic symptoms of conflicting enablers that are roughly in balance. The immediate consequence is *corporate power play*. This is probably the unintended side effect that people are most commonly aware of, although in reality corporate camouflage tends to be the more prevalent of the side effects caused by balanced conflicts, and each of the side effects caused by weaker conflicts are even more common.

Power play is often far more subtle than a clash of egos. It is, after all, the result of trying to balance conflicting enablers. Indeed, it has often been institutionalized. Many multinationals exhibit chronic power play because of matrix organizations they adopted in the 1970s. The unwritten rule becomes: "Keep your *chosen* boss happy." You see the same phenomenon with functions versus processes, technical experts versus line management, and local versus corporate computer networks.

Still more complex power play is necessary when dealing with enablers comprising many people, for example fellow researchers in an R&D lab who judge the value of your work, or peers in an organization where anyone can veto a budget. There you have to remain on good terms with a large number of individuals, each of whom may deliberately or inadvertently be pushing in conflicting directions.

When power play becomes too extreme because of unclear roles or differing management styles, the side effect degenerates into *corporate civil war*. Then, the whole organization spends more time and energy fighting itself than the competition. Guess what happens to them next?

From Conspiracy to Treachery

Corporate power games and corporate civil war do not disappear just because somebody bangs heads together. Instead, they become more insidious, more dangerous, more damaging.

Specific situations where a new enabler is forced through, despite being in strong conflict with existing enablers, create the unintended side effect of *corporate conspiracy*. Typical examples would be somebody given authority over someone who strongly disliked them, or an acquired company after a hostile takeover, or a corporate information system imposed from above, or two battling department heads told by their CEO that they have to cooperate, or a charismatic or authoritarian leader insisting her direct reports do something they do not believe in.

Under these circumstances, it's usually considered inappropriate to fight openly. So, out come the daggers, and as soon as everyone's backs are turned, in they all go. Or else people say one thing and then appear disloyal because they do something else. Sometimes everyone appears very civilized, but they follow the same approach as a shop assistant dealing with an unpleasant customer who nevertheless can complain and get them fired: "I'm very sorry, Sir, but I'm afraid that company policy is quite strict on this point. My hands are tied. Have a nice day."

In some organizations, corporate conspiracy no longer results from a few isolated undercover power struggles. Instead, enablers conflict throughout the organization and power politics is endemic. The side effect that then develops is *corporate treachery*. Trust is not, shall we say, as strong as it could be. Personal attacks, behind people's backs, are the norm and anonymous tip offs can ruin your promotion chances without you even hearing about them. Surprisingly, some of these organizations are also, apparently, our most respectable: elite clubs at which government, financial, and legal institutions are all represented as is the art world, academia, even the secret services and the military. Of course, some of these play a major role in all of our lives ... Woops!

From Lipservice to Cynicism

When we consider conflicts with motivators, we're back to basics. We're dealing with what is important to people: what they perceive as valuable rewards or as undesirable penalties. Enablers and triggers serve no purpose unless they are linked to motivators. But there are many levels of motivators. An individual may, for example, want exciting work and money. But for her to get those she may need to gain rapid promotion and of course keep her job; both of which are subsidiary motivators.

The motivators within an organization are really a further detailing of the famous Maslow hierarchy of human needs; a motivator like "having a job" only feels important when there is a threat you may lose it. Occasionally, people are quite clear about their order of priorities: The sales division of a major computer company once insisted to me that their true motivators were food, sex, and commission ...

When an organization tries to make changes that affect the degree to which people's motivators are satisfied—or tries to encourage new motivators—there is great potential for conflict. Relatively weak attempts to get employees to value quality, teamwork, cross-functional cooperation, business focus, or environmental issues all run the risk that they do not correspond to what actually feels important to the majority involved. This leads to *corporate lipservice*. On the surface people agree. They may genuinely agree—intellectually. But day-to-day it does not feel important and does not fit the existing unwritten rules.

When too many people pay too much lipservice too often, things degenerate into *corporate cynicism*. Managers adopt a "do as I say, not as I do" attitude, fueling the cynicism still further. Frustration builds because of successive failures to introduce changes to motivators that do not tie in with existing enablers and triggers. Employees intuitively test any new initiative against the existing unwritten rules and, finding it does not fit, gripe: "It'll never work!" And they're right.

From Subversion
to Torture

I have lost track of the number of vision statements that CEOs have proudly shown me as the outcome from a weekend retreat in Malibu. Some are good. Too many look like this: "We will be the leading organization in our selected field. We will work in partnership to be the quality supplier of choice to our customers while providing a rewarding occupation to our employees. In so doing we will realize attractive returns for our investors. We will be responsible members of our community and will do nothing to injure our environment." Sometimes, but not always, there is the additional phrase: "We will be particularly kind to old ladies and small animals."

They do not mean anything. They sound good but in practice they probably fly in the face of a whole host of unwritten rules that reinforce motivators such as power, individualism, and status. Unless the vision statements are carefully crafted to reflect existing motivators and unwritten rules, or else have a hidden migration path underpinning them, then they are just grandiose words "full of sound and fury, signifying nothing."

The problems come when such vision statements are enforced. Then the only recourse is *corporate subversion*. People talk of the importance of personal computers but make sure they work on the high-prestige super mainframe project. They talk about incremental improvement but seek the high-profile "quantum leaps." Managers say they value depth of experience, but they keep job hopping anyway.

When there are too many balanced but conflicting motivators, an organization sinks into *corporate torture*. People are torn between conflicting values. They want to remain research specialists but know that the only way they can get more exciting work is to generalize. They believe in the benefits of empowerment but they like the feeling of being in direct charge. They are ambitious but they also want quality of life with their young family. No one can perform well for long like that.

From Sabotage to Suicide

Of all the side effects caused by naive introduction of changes to an organization, the ones described here are the most painful, the most damaging, the most hidden, the most unforgivable. None is worse. Some of the most depressing conversations of my career have been with people trapped in organizations where major changes were forced through in flagrant contravention of people's true motivators. Of course, during massive downsizing or business reorientation, it's very difficult not to hurt some people. And the most common phrase I hear at the moment regarding reengineering is: "You can't make an omelet without breaking eggs." The trouble is that the side effect that occurs whenever change initiatives are driven in strong conflict with motivators is *corporate sabotage*. People's true values do not change under duress. Even under exigencies of war, where some pretty nasty approaches have been tried, no one has ever been able to change what was really important to people through force. Instead, resistance goes underground.

People feel that their moral contract with the organization has been broken, so they wait their chance. And as soon as market conditions are right the best leave—not through attrition but in droves—resulting in a band of mediocrity remaining. Those who cannot escape are "in it for themselves." So, if the CEO's initiative crashes, then "it serves her right."

No organization can survive long if it is consistently undermined from within. Too great a gulf between espoused and real motivators is unbridgeable. If top managers are not sophisticated enough to satisfy people's existing motivators in a new way, or else compensate by satisfying previously unaddressed motivators, then they and their organization are on the slippery slope to oblivion. Their organization will soon be in the death throws of *corporate suicide*. Most people within the body of the organization will still mourn its pasing—not because of what it became but because of their lost jobs and because of what it once was. But, since it degraded to a tyranny, it's better off dead.

I think we need to hold a mirror up to our organization.

4
The Road to Pragmatism

Don't Push Me!

Question: Whose fault is it when people act in the unprofessional ways outlined in the last nine sections? Who should you blame?

Answer: It is nobody's fault. You should blame no one.

The whole point of the unwritten rules of the game is that many of us would act in identical ways under similar circumstances given the same unwritten rules. They are what genuinely feel like the sensible ways to behave. Some people's motivators are different from our own, and so they may interpret the rules differently from us. But you cannot blame them for that. And if we do share the same broad motivators as the other people in our organization, then the chances are we would interpret the unwritten rules at their level in the same ways as they do, and act accordingly—all the way to corporate conspiracy and sabotage.

When we analyze the unwritten rules and uncover some unsavory unintended negative side effects, we are not rooting out unprofessionalism—we are simply highlighting the inherent though unintentional hypocrisy that has been built into the existing written rules. And the conflicts are often far from obvious. They come from policies, procedures, and management actions that are not apparently even related to each other. What's more, intuition often doesn't hold true anymore as a means of understanding the relationships. So, even the most intelligent and compassionate manager cannot be expected to see the links unaided. There's no blame there either.

Even when top executives apparently mismanage their business and force through changes that are in conflict with motivators, enablers, and triggers and create hidden problems and store up risk for the future, there's no blame, because I've never yet met a top executive who realized the damage that he or she was actually causing. I've never yet found a CEO who realized the implications of the progression shown in the matrix below; who recognized the peril of pushing an initiative too hard without the sophistication to make it "fit." None of us recognized it.

Perceived pressure from the new initiative compared with existing conflicting unwritten rules	SIDE EFFECTS CAUSED BY CONFLICTS		
WEAKER	Lipservice CYNICISM	Isolation IMPOTENCE	Rebellion ANARCHY
BALANCED	Subversion TORTURE	Power play CIVIL WAR	Camouflage GRIDLOCK
STRONGER	Sabotage SUICIDE	Conspiracy TREACHERY	Paranoia PANIC
	MOTIVATORS	ENABLERS	TRIGGERS

Derivation of those unwritten rules
that conflict with the initiative

But that is where the blamelessness ends.

When managers realize what is going on, when they appreciate the consequences of a gung-ho attitude to forcing their policies through regardless, when they recognize the unnecessary barriers to performance, the unnecessary pain and trauma that they are inflicting on their organization and still not achieving their desired goals—and they nevertheless continue—then the blame is all theirs. And their willful negligence is tantamount to management malpractice.

That is the reason that I so facetiously refered to their behavior as *Macho Lemming Syndrome* earlier in this book. That is why I'm so scathing of managers who are imperious and uncompassionate. That is why my most damning indictments are of executives who tell me they believe that "sometimes you need to create a bit of pain in an organization just to pep things up a bit," or "sometimes you need to just tell people what they *will* do and don't waste time discussing it" and then they send the painful message by memo rather than walking down the corridor and conveying the message face to face. That is why I'm always so tempted to respond to them: "If you can't stand the need to empathize get out of the way of those who can—you've become a liability."

The ultimate grounds for rejecting their approach to management is not because of all the unnecessary stress and discomfort within an organization that their philosophy engenders—although in an ideal world that would be sufficient—the justification for choosing a different path is simply that their approach *does not work any more*. In today's rapidly changing environment, with the need for inherent flexibility and constant change, there's no time for the unintended negative side effects that their approach sets up to work their way out of the system.

In the past we could impose changes that created conflicts, but then wait for the tensions in the system to be resolved. People left. People gradually changed their attitudes. People slowly recognized the inherent conflicts between specific policies and procedures and resolved them. But we do not have that luxury any more. We are not heading for a new steady state. We are heading for wave upon wave of new change. So, if we use the old style of management to push our change initiatives through we build up wave upon wave of unintended side effects. These side effects themselves then combine and reinforce, at different rates in different parts of the organization, creating still more unintended side effects, whose derivations are now massively convoluted. That is exactly the situation we have found in companies claiming to suffer from "change fatigue." The fatigue—an inability to effect further sustainable change—results from a saturation of unresolved side effects.

So the only solution is to unravel what's going on. To do that, you need to do more than just recognize the broad types of side effects in your organization. You need to understand exactly what's causing them so, at last, you can swing aside the barriers to business performance.

Swinging Aside the Barriers

Let's take stock of what we have so far.

A new wave of management thinking is spreading worldwide. The overriding theme is improving business performance by changing the ways people behave. But that's something that few managers feel at home with. Many believe that they need a new core management skill, but most don't know exactly what it is.

The skill that we all need is to understand—and if necessary to change—the unwritten rules of the game within our organizations. The unwritten rules can open or close the gates to better business performance.

But management actions and changes to written rules—relating to strategy, processes, resources, and organization—cannot directly affect performance. People interpret them in the light of various factors such as national and regional cultural expectations, the economic climate, regulation, legislation, private agendas, and existing unwritten rules.

The net result is a set of unwritten rules that drives corporate behavior, and so performance, directly. So, for managers trying to implement actions to improve their business (such as total quality, process reengineering, learning organization), the unwritten rules act as the gatekeepers to success by encouraging or blocking the improvement. Mastery of the unwritten rules of the game is the core skill that the new wave manager needs to swing aside the barriers to business performance.

Within companies, most employees absorb rather than learn the unwritten rules. But you *can* analyze and codify them in an unambiguous way. In all such analyses, my colleagues at Arthur D. Little and I have found that large groups within a given organization often share the same unwritten rules—although those rules may be very different from those of another organization.

At first sight, you may find that the unwritten rules of an organization appear to be encouraging the behavior management is seeking. Often, however, something is being garbled in the translation and the unwritten rules are producing unintended side effects and conflicts that result in barriers to high performance. For example, a need for individual profile within the organization may be damaging team-work, or pressure to job hop every few years may be encouraging chronic short-termism.

So far so good. We've got all the recapitulation out of the way. Now we can concentrate on how you can hold the mirror up to your own organization and uncover and codify its unwritten rules.

The rules of the game appraisal technique that is detailed in the guide at the back of this book has proven the most readily teachable approach of many I have tried. My colleagues and I have used it with great success since the late 1980s. Many managers have subsequently learned to apply the technique for themselves. More recent develop-ments now allow us to guide the process with greater precision, and gather stronger indications of just what changes should be made to written rules and management actions. However, so far, these new techniques seem to require far more experience and judgment to work successfully, and as such are not readily transferrable skills. The tried and trusted methodology in this book is far more helpful if you want to uncover and codify the unwritten rules of your organization—when, like most people, you've never done it before.

The appraisal is designed to bring to the surface the main unwritten rules *that relate to specific business issues.* Using it, you will not uncover *all* the unwritten rules of the game within your organization. Indeed, why would you want to? Instead, you will find primarily only the unwritten rules that result in potentially negative and positive side effects affecting selected aspects of business performance.

But how do you know the specific business issues for which an unwritten rules appraisal is likely to be most relevant? Particularly as some business problems often don't appear related to unwritten rules at all: "We don't know the direction the market will develop," or "We need a new strategy." As a rule of thumb, the unwritten rules tend to be far more immediately relevant to questions relating to process rather than questions of content. So, "Why do we never seem to know which way the market develops?" or "How can we improve our finger on the pulse of the market?" may both have strong unwritten rule components. Whereas, "What direction will the market develop?" probably will not.

The effort involved in the appraisal depends on how many different sets of unwritten rules you're addressing. If you're dealing with an organization that has a high diversity of unwritten rules then you could use the methodology to codify the rules for many or all of the different groups, all at the same time. That could take several weeks or even months. Often, though, it's far more practical to conduct a pilot appraisal within a group that all share broadly the same unwritten rules. For such a group, you can, if necessary, uncover the main unwritten rules relating to specific business issues within five days.

As explained earlier in the book, you in essence conduct an appraisal by answering three sets of questions:

1. What are the motivators and associated unwritten rules? (*What* is important to people, and so how do they act?)

2. What are the enablers and associated unwritten rules? (Given the motivators, *who* is important to people, and so how do they act?)

3. What are the triggers and associated unwritten rules? (Given the motivators and enablers, *how* are people actually measured, and so how do they act?)

The answers to these questions, and their implications for behavior, lead you to the unwritten rules of the game for that environment and the logic implicit in behavior that may be working against high performance.

However, few people within an organization are accustomed to thinking about their behavior in terms of these three questions. And even if they were, they would nevertheless tend to be cautious about sharing the more sensitive answers with anyone—especially with anyone from their own organization. To do so often makes people feel Machiavellian. And few people want to be *perceived* as Machiavellian.

As an aside, I think poor old Machiavelli has received really bad press. The more I learn about him the more he turns out to have been a really great guy. All he did was dare to write down some of the unwritten rules of the game of Renaissance Italy and then publish them in a book called *The Prince*. It was, admittedly, a little unfortunate that he chose the aristocracy as his initial target population to study because most of their unwritten rules at one stage or another involved murdering people. But that wasn't Machiavelli's fault. He was just recording what he found. I think modern historians should recast him as one of the pioneers of unwritten rules of the game theory.

Anyway, responding to such vagaries of history, the modern day unwritten rules appraisal is designed to encourage people to open up. It also guides you in structuring what they tell you in the interviews. It's all a bit like putting an organization onto the psychoanalyst's couch ...

Just Lie Back on the Couch...

You can codify the unwritten rules through a carefully constructed sequence of two-hour interviews. The sequence itself is detailed in the guide at the back of this book. But who should be interviewed? What combination will allow you to get away with the smallest number of interviews, and so cause the least amount of disruption? When I first started unwritten rules analyses, I thought that the ideal interview slice would be a diagonal throughout the organization. However, my colleagues and I rapidly found that we then needed several interviews simply to disentangle the differing perspectives that occur at the different levels of a traditional hierarchy.

Over the last several years we've found that—in the absence of indicators to the contrary—the most productive source of interviewees tends to be a horizontal slice of middle managers: They often feel caught between a rock and a hard place and they *have* to understand and live by the unwritten rules. So, if you have to choose one subset of the business where the inherent conflicts of written rules, management actions, and new change initiatives will show themselves strongest, then the middle levels of the organization you are studying is your best starting place.

As for interviewers, ideally you should have two: one leading the interview, and the other in support. Only when an interview is very sensitive is it better to have only one interviewer. But who should you choose to conduct the interviews? Can you ever uncover the unwritten rules within your own organization? Or do you always have to resort to using outsiders?

I learned the answers to these questions the hard way. I remember a few years ago being dragged, kicking and screaming, into a rules of the game analysis for one of Arthur D. Little's larger clients. The client was insisting that one of its employees be present at every interview to confirm what the interviewees said to us "outside consultants." Not only was their spy to be from the same corporation as the interviewees, but also from the same division, indeed from the same business unit. I predicted disaster. I ranted about camouflage, wasted effort, and "big brother," but to no avail. Against my better judgment I grudgingly accepted the challenge to try conducting a pilot appraisal, using an employee of the organization as my support interviewer. "But, no promises!"

I resolved that although my hands might be tied, I could at least ensure that they were not tied behind my back. So I insisted on carefully selecting the partner myself. I was given a choice of two people. After great deliberation I flipped a coin and chose a member of the business unit's Change Management task force. Thanks to the last minute rescheduling of the first interview, the planned training program had to be curtailed. Basically, we had about two minutes. I adopted one of my less verbose briefings: "Why don't you just sit there, say nothing, and take lots and lots of notes." As this did not appear to convey the full depth of confidence that I was trying to instil, I thought a bit more, and added: "You'll be great!" and followed up with an encouraging smile. Sixty seconds later we walked into the office of our first interviewee. I beamed and shook hands. "This," I thought, "shows the potential of becoming one of those absolute, unmitigated disasters that destroy otherwise promising careers ..."

Everything was a tremendous success. Not only did that first interview go well, with the interviewee opening up and uncovering some marvelous insights about how the company really operated, but so did all the other interviews. What's more, after each interview my friendly spy was able to fill in details that explained specific biases and quirks that had been apparent during the meeting. Each interviewee was assured that nothing they said would be attributed to them in any feedback to top management. Nobody held back. On the contrary, they seemed spurred on by the fact that they could open up with complete immunity to a fellow employee. Far from being an insurmountable liability, my support interviewer rapidly became a major asset. No one felt the need to hold back in front of him because he was seen as being impartial, detached from the mainstream line structure, with no axe to grind on his own account. With hindsight, he was a very lucky choice.

Since then, I have rarely conducted an unwritten rules of the game appraisal *without* using a member of the client company as my partner—either in the role of support or, once they were trained, as lead. The lesson my colleagues and I learned is that one or both interviewers can be selected from the organization being appraised, *provided that you and they judge that the interviewees will not be intimidated.* Having insiders involved encourages far greater ownership of the findings, as well as providing opportunities for skills transfer throughout the organization. Of course, you cannot use just anybody. Choose wrongly, and the findings from the whole appraisal can be hopelessly skewed. But, carefully selecting appropriate interviewers from the organization being appraised is an excellent investment.

What's more, despite worries about not being able to see the wood for the trees, it does not appear to be all that difficult to conduct an unwritten rules appraisal of your own organization. In the late 1980s we started conducting unwritten rules of the game appraisals on ourselves at Arthur D. Little. I conducted the early ones. There were no problems, despite my being part of the organization. But then, so we told ourselves, I was supposed to be reasonably competent in the technique. The next appraisal involved some of my colleagues as interviewers. Again, no problems. When a major client conducted a perfectly adequate appraisal using its own people as interviewers, we finally conceded defeat and gave up all pretensions that external consultants were a prerequisite to uncovering unwritten rules.

Although it would be wonderfully self serving to suggest the contrary, you *can* often conduct a perfectly adequate initial appraisal of your organization's unwritten rules—yourself. External support may be helpful to get people to open up, as a source of comparison with other appraisals, to put your findings within a broader context such as process reengineering or total quality, or to guide you on which changes to your written rules and management behaviors are most likely to prove successful and sustainable. But before seeking advice from a physician, try a home diagnosis. Once you understand what's really causing you pain, you may find that the cure is obvious.

If you want to learn how you can conduct an unwritten rules appraisal, you'll find detailed instructions in the guide at the end of this book. In an emergency, a colleague of mine from our Houston office took a draft of the guide with him to Argentina, and with no other training conducted a highly successful unwritten rules appraisal in a foreign language. I can't imagine a much more severe test than that.

Armed with the methodology detailed in the guide, you can gather the evidence needed to show what to change in your own organization. You can find the rules that are causing problems and break them. You can take on a new role, a new persona. When a rule gives pain; when you want to change; who ya gonna call? RULEBUSTERS!

Members of the Board, it gives me great pleasure to introduce our new Vice President for Change Management ...

5
Call
RULEBUSTERS

Rulebusting

If you want to break the rules you need to understand them first. As far as I'm aware, the only practical reason for conducting an unwritten rules analysis is to use the findings to help guide you to change some of the rules and so improve performance. That is the context in which top management should discuss the evidence gathered during an appraisal. An example of the output from an appraisal is included at the end of the RULEBUSTER's Guide at the back of this book. A word of caution though: Not everyone finds it easy to internalize feedback from the rules of the game. People tend to work through different reactions before eventual acceptance. Indeed, one of my multinational oil company clients insists on calling this whole process of acceptance: "Sarah."

I assumed they were just being cute. How nice, I thought, to be on first name terms with a change process. Only after several months did one of the directors point out that SARAH was an acronym. After a bit of prodding, he vaguely remembered it stood for: Shock, Anger, Rejection, Acceptance, and so Hope. Very neat, and pretty accurate. I'm sure they borrowed it from some consultant somewhere. But no one I asked could remember whom.

Anyway, give people at least three days grace between detailed feedback and any discussion about what to do next. Then the first item for discussion should be whether you all feel you have enough information to propose changes. You should agree whether the appraisal should be extended to cover extra populations, a diagonal slice of the business or perhaps to uncover further barriers or catalysts to performance. You should also evaluate the need to corroborate any perceived damage caused by side effects. For instance, employees may believe that the company's introspective focus is damaging customers' perceptions of service quality, but maybe it simply isn't true.

If no further investigation is deemed necessary, you should next set up a top-management workshop. The agenda is as follows:

TOP MANAGEMENT WORKSHOP

1) <u>Prioritize</u> the perceived business risks or potential opportunities from side effects highlighted by the unwritten rules of the game analysis.

2) Agree on exactly <u>what behavior</u> we want in place of what we currently have.

3) Use our understanding of cause and effect between written rules, unwritten rules and side effects to indicate appropriate changes to written rules.

Be warned—keep the invitation list to the workshop *short*: ideally about five top managers. Never allow yourself to be persuaded to have more than 10 people in the room. A major insurance company recently cajolled me into running the workshop with 20 participants. I don't want to talk about it ...

Even when the group is small enough to be constructive, however, the three innocent agenda items just listed can happily fill a day. The first item is a necessary filter. Although, throughout the analysis, the interviewers will have used their business judgment to focus on the more important side effects, there still may be too many. Anyway, not all perceived negative side effects are equally damaging. Some may be quite acceptable. Or some may be acceptable in isolation, but not in the company of others.

You need to rank the risks and opportunities. You are not interested in removing every possible negative side effect. It's not worth the effort. Any organization can withstand a certain amount of conflict. However, you may find that you can do a classic Pareto analysis on the side effects and select the 20 percent that cause 80 percent of the damage.

You don't need to be overly scientific about your selection, but some companies and some cultures do like to try. I remember once having a European client who loved to see everything quantified. We ran the top-management workshop with the assistance of computer programs that took various rankings provided by the group, ran all kinds of weird and wonderful statistical packages, and spewed forth the results onto color monitors around the room. It was great fun and provided a spurious credibility to the rankings that, in reality, were no more or less subjective than if we had conducted the process on the back of an envelope. But the managers adored it and felt far more confident because a computer was in the loop. Whatever works.

The second agenda item requires you to construct a vision of how you want your company to be in the future. Not the company vision statement—you need to be more specific than that.

For example, what if the unwritten rules analysis has indicated that strong pressure for functions to protect their own turf is damaging cross-functional cooperation across the business? Fine, what do you want in its place? You do *not* want everybody spending all of their time on grandiose cross-functional business wide issues. The functions are probably very good at doing what they're good at. You don't want to lose that. So, what is the trade off? In practice, what do you want cross-functional cooperation to look like? You must go through the same soul searching for each of the side effects that you want to change.

The final agenda item calls for the greatest creativity. Certainly, the more times that you do it, the easier it gets. The rest of this book is aimed at offering some help, based on experience built up over several years.

You can start with any "burning solutions" that arose during the appraisal to suggest changes to written rules and management actions that would impact the motivators, enablers, and triggers in appropriate ways. Examples of how other organizations have tackled similar problems may be a useful starting point, and the following two parts of this book cover a number.

But be warned. As I said before, we have all learned from what happened a few years ago. Some people thought you could describe corporate excellence and, through copying such organizations, become excellent yourself. But what works for one organization will not necessarily work for another—even if on the surface the two organizations look similar. It sometimes does not even work between divisions of the same company. So let's not pretend that there are too many solutions to achieving high performance that are common across all companies.

But one thing may be common, at least to most organizations: the ways to break down the barriers to high performance—or, should I say, the different versions of high performance. The best description that I know of what high-performance businesses of the future will look like is not in terms of *what* they end up looking like but in terms of *how* they actually get there. To understand how best to interpret their lessons, we need to understand the nature of change itself.

User's guide to trauma

Everybody's talking about change these days. Everybody's using the same word, but everybody does not use the word to mean the same thing. Even when it comes to major change, people using the word "reengineering," use it to mean different things.

Worse, some consultants and change agents have started to abuse the term "paradigm shift." When Thomas Kuhn coined the term in 1970 as a way of describing scientific revolution, it was meant to encapsulate the notion that when you have a particular mindset— such as Newtonian mechanics—you are likely to misinterpret experimental data so that it fits your mental model. Only when empirical observation conflicts too much with that model are you likely to change paradigms to a new mental model—say, quantum mechanics. Now people are starting to use paradigm shift as synonymous with "big change." Rubbish. You can go through major corporate upheaval but keep exactly the same paradigm. The whole point is that they are *not* the same. The next time someone misuses the term to you, register that they really don't know what on earth they're talking about. Buyer beware.

So what is change? Well, although there's a whole spectrum of different kinds of change, my colleagues and I have found it very useful to distinguish three types. Each of them requires a different amount of effort and in our experience offers different levels of improvement over time.

The most common form of improvement is *incremental*—evolutionary, one step at a time. Total quality management (TQM) has become the most common banner for this type of change. It's attractive because you get results quickly. It's often very successful at the departmental level and within functions. And most organizations these days, at least in the business sector, are rather good at getting the improvements at this level. However, TQM, in the incremental sense that most companies define it, has not in general managed to live up to its promise of generating fundamental improvements.

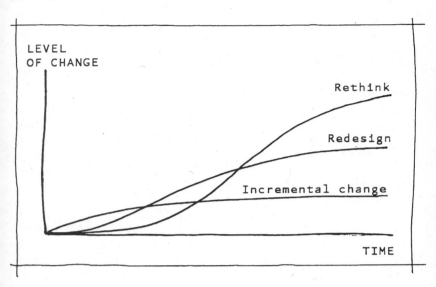

Some companies insist to me that they're different because they mean *total* quality. Strange, I thought that TQM by definition meant total quality. Anyway, what I guess they're trying to say is that they don't view TQM as just incremental. Indeed, many are claiming that reengineering is also part of their TQM initiative. Fine. They're choosing to redefine the term so as not to lose momentum of an initiative that, all too often, would otherwise rapidly stall for lack of sustained and sustainable deliverables. But that loses the benefit of distinguishing incremental improvement techniques from the rest. Incremental approaches are good in their place. As tools for change they have overwhelmingly proven necessary—but not sufficient.

If incremental approaches such as narrow interpretations of TQM are not adequate, then what else can we do? First, we can *redesign*. This technique came to the fore in the 1980s when everybody started to use computers to automate what they were doing. To begin with, people tended simply to automate the same old ways of doing things, complete with all the old inefficiencies, illogicalities, and ineffectiveness.

As an example, I remember being very confused at why members of a particular department in a company seemed to write everything down for the department head. They wrote even when a phone call would do or a brief chat in the hall. And this had resulted in enormous numbers of forms and unnecessary protocol. So, I wondered if people there were simply paranoid. Were they covering their backs, or were they just naturally bureaucratic?

It turned out that the real reason was that 15 years earlier, the then head of department unfortunately had been an extraordinarily long and slow communicator. The simplest reply could turn into a speech of epic proportions. Simple sentences were delivered in a painfully protracted idiom punctuated by apparently random pauses of several seconds, usually in the very middle of sentences. Often these would lead to spontaneous diversions onto irrelevant topics that could last up to half an hour. Inexperienced juniors were sometimes caught unawares and trapped for the rest of the day.

So, over the years, in an attempt to reduce the massive timelags between asking a simple question and getting a meaningful response, the whole department had resorted to a form of dialogue by proxy. And that was what I was seeing. The original cause had been formalized and seemingly set in concrete. And that is typical of the weird reasons why old processes have evolved as they have.

It was examples like that that led software engineers to start redesigning processes. In other words, they planned how to streamline the ways things were done, to reflect new technologies and ways for doing things, and then they automated the redesigned activities. As an example, over the last ten years many companies have redesigned their product development and manufacturing activities by applying simultaneous engineering approaches to shorten leadtimes.

Redesign takes longer than incremental improvement, but the scale of improvement may be higher. Yet even redesigning processes does not offer the quantum leaps that some organizations are looking for. For these, you may need to *rethink* as well. Go back to the drawing board, ask why activities exist at all, and then come up with a better way of achieving the same goal. You may even decide to change the goal. A classic example was the transition over a decade ago from the conventional wisdom on inventory management to the radical concept of Just-In-Time. The more radical forms of business process reengineering fall into the category of rethink. Rethinking takes time to translate into benefits. In the end, though, the benefits are potentially far higher than with any other approach *however long you stick at it*. Provided, of course, you are able to reap those benefits. Ah, there's the problem.

Life after change

We keep coming back to it. It is what I think of as the *dilemma of change*: Major change offers the greatest potential benefits but carries by far the greatest likelihood of failure. Why?

The answer lies in the scope of change, rather than the amount of change. Let me explain. As you move up the spectrum from incremental improvement to redesign and to rethink, so you end up changing more and more different aspects of the business. With incremental improvement, you may change a manufacturing process or an accounting process, or you may modify the bonus scheme, or introduce a new computer system, or refine your strategy. When you rethink, you need to change all of them, all at the same time. The boundary, the scope, of what you are doing is far larger.

And that means that you have to recognize the implications and repercussions of each of the changes on the others. You can no longer view different aspects of your change in isolation. It's like a doctor looking after a patient. She has to take a holistic view. She must look at the big picture. She has to recognize the likely side effects of one drug interacting with another. She has to compensate for the effects on an illness when operating on the patient to remove the original cause. There is no such thing as an academically neat surgical procedure. "The operation was a success but the patient died" is not, in practice, acceptable.

Corporate change is no different. There too we need the holistic view. That, of course, is one of the reasons why the unwritten rules of the game provide such a helpful insight. Being the net effect of all of the various aspects of the business, analyzing the unwritten rules highlights any misalignment of the different parts of the business.

So, how can we tie motivators, enablers, and triggers into the big picture. In fact, wait a moment, what does this famous big picture actually look like?

Easy approaches to holism

No one in their right mind goes around suggesting to top managers that they should change triggers or modify an enabler. The point is that, vital as the concepts of motivators, enablers, and triggers are, they're not the jargon of day-to-day management. Not yet anyway. So we need not only to tie them into everyday terminology, but also relate them to every aspect of an organization.

There are an infinite number of ways of classifying a business. There are even an infinite number of ways of doing it correctly. It doesn't really matter what you use. But of the wide variety of models being hawked at the moment, I almost hesitate to admit that I find that the best is the one developed by my colleagues at Arthur D. Little. "Well he would say that wouldn't he!" Well, actually "No he wouldn't," because my instinct says to come up with something better. But I do find the model very useful. See what you think. At first glance the model is deceptively simple. It shows the interrelationships of only four key aspects of a dynamic organization:

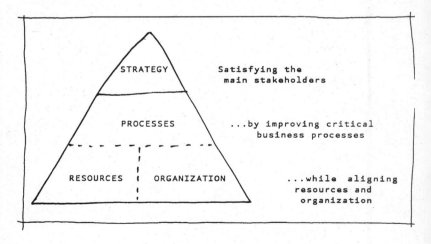

Stakeholders and strategies—how the organization chooses to satisfy everyone with a vested interest in the business, from customers, employees, and owners, to suppliers and the community.

Processes—the important ones are now recognized as being far broader than narrow functional procedures because they determine how the business mobilizes all its resources to meet the stakeholder needs.

Resources—including information and people.

Organization—including structure and management techniques.

Aligning the four aspects of the model is all that any high performance business has to do. Easy, huh? We'll see.

One of the reasons that I find this model so much more helpful than others is because it ties high performance back to balancing the needs of different stakeholders, deciding how to resolve the inevitable conflicts between those needs, and making sure that they're all integrated into strategies. But this explicit balancing of stakeholder needs is far from trivial. In fact, it's extraordinary how often organizations have never even fully considered it. Frequently, they've not even considered what the various needs of all the different types of stakeholder really are.

After all, there are owners (equity, pension funds, controlling families, institutions, banks, governments), employees (professional, field staff, clerical, top management, production, sales, full-timers, part-timers, men, women, young, old), customers (retail, secretaries ordering for their bosses, distributors, children watching TV ads and influencing their parents), suppliers (of goods, raw materials, components, energy, advice, services, know-how), and community in the widest sense (local region, environmental aspects at plant and customer level, support of local small businesses, political involvement). Each of these needs may be different. Each has to be explicitly addressed, and then disregarded. The tradeoffs of each conflicting need then have to be decided and reflected into strategy. They hardly ever are. No surprise under those circumstances that the unwritten rules driving the company are not all optimally aligned either. How could they be?

But for the strategies to succeed, a company's key processes must also be efficient and effective and aligned with the stakeholder needs. That's the next potential stumbling block: more grounds to expect misalignment in unwritten rules and therefore barriers to performance. Nevertheless, it has proven very useful to think in terms of key business processes that tend to stretch across businesses, simply because they do cross functions, or sites, or both. It's in the management of the interactions and tradeoffs that the biggest opportunities for improvement lie, now that most individual departments and functions have been streamlined and improved. Most of the key business processes, however, will never have been considered as a whole before—often because only the CEO has the authority to do so. Yet, as explained before, the sprawling nature of business processes is a double-edged sword. It offers great potential but also invokes the *dilemma of change* because so much needs to be changed at once.

Not only do stakeholder needs all have to be deliberately balanced, and processes aligned to that strategy, but corporate resources and organization also have to be set up in ways that optimally support all the processes. Now we're starting to see the enormity of the task of balancing that big picture. Resources include people, facilities, information, technology, and so on. Managing our resources is hardly a new idea. But the new skill required is to manage them not just to support business functions, but also to underpin the key processes. Once again, everything needs to be aligned.

Finally, there's great scope for reassessing organization structure and management techniques once we view our business from the perspective of processes rather than functions. In some ways, it's about time. Our modern organization structure is not actually all that modern. How old? A century? A few hundred years? Back to the dawn of the industrial revolution? A thousand years?

Well, it all really stems back to Alexander the Great a few thousand years ago. His armies were the first documented example of the now classic hierarchical structure. When he invaded a new country he wanted all his armies to follow his master plan. At a time when cellular phones and faxes were in depressingly short supply, the last thing old Alexander needed was for one of his generals to say, "I see a better way of doing it" and go off and do his own thing. So the whole structure was designed to prevent lateral communication and to stifle innovation and change. Unfortunately, these are the very things that these days we all go around saying we want to encourage.

Now you see why balancing the stakeholder needs and strategies with the processes, resources, and organization is so terribly difficult. Yet we all intuitively know it's vital to get that alignment. In which case, where is the measure for alignment of strategy, processes, resources, and organization? After all, we can't improve what we can't measure ...

Better business made simple

The performance indicator for alignment of stakeholder needs and strategy, processes, resources, and organization is the unwritten rules of the game analysis. What else could it be? The unwritten rules are themselves the net effect of all the different management levers in a business. So any misalignments in the levers will show themselves, via the unwritten rules, as unintended negative side effects.

It's impossible to conceive of an organization in which you had misalignment that did not show up in the unwritten rules analysis. If the balance of stakeholder needs specified by the strategy is out of alignment with the processes intended to satisfy them, or the resources and organization are not fully aligned with supporting the processes, then these inevitably create unintended negative side effects. Using the unwritten rules as the missing link in your understanding, you can locate the side effects and then track back to what's causing them.

But think about that a bit more. It's not just that the unwritten rules analysis can act as a performance indicator of the overall alignment of a business—it is the *only* universal indicator of alignment. Even measures of overall business performance, such as profitability or market share, only indicate consequences of alignment or misalignment. They're not measuring alignment directly. And so they can provide little or no guidance when something is going wrong. Taken the other way around, if you look at the unwritten rules in your organization and do not find any unintended negative side effects, then that is as good a definition of alignment as I know. Lack of major negative side effects is the prerequisite condition for achieving high performance.

Strategy, processes, resources, and organization each have motivator, enabler, and trigger components. In the next three sections, we'll at last see how they all tie together and what impact this has.

U make my day

Motivators correspond to employee needs, and these days they increasingly tend to be strongly reflected in strategy. Motivators can also be heavily impacted by process descriptions, resource allocation, and organization. Misalignment of any of these can cause conflicts with motivators. You can resolve such conflicts by satisfying the same motivators in a new way, by satisfying new motivators in place of the old, or by selecting people with different motivators. You're very unlikely to change people's motivators by only attacking them head on.

Strategy

Conflicts with Motivators

Classic conflicts occur when an organization fundamentally changes direction. When a research division decides that it must become more responsive to its internal customers, employees who joined the company expecting a career on the cutting edge of research find themselves forced to conduct medium-term development work instead. Likewise, an organization moving into a lean and mean industry like computer disk drives, may find too great a change in motivators required for it to work.

Potential Solutions

Inadequate skills can be corrected by training; inappropriate motivators cannot. If a change in strategy is too extreme, the only recourse may be to replace existing employees with those who have motivators that fit the new strategy better; inevitably, though, this raises serious questions about the logic behind the new strategy. Sometimes you can rechannel people's motivators. For example, many researchers have risen to the intellectual challenge of managing commercial tradeoffs in their work.

Processes

Conflicts with Motivators

Since the industrial revolution, process descriptions have risked turning humans into slaves for machines. Whether on the factory floor or in the administration department, it's all too easy for processes to conflict with our true motivators. Sometimes, though, whole industries adopt processes that are aligned with one group's motivators but in conflict with another group's. In the film industry, actors, agents, directors, and writers all want movies to be as large budget as possible—the accountants don't.

Potential Solutions

Industrial automation has long been studied to better understand how to balance processes to reflect the needs of employees. More recently the techniques have been applied to clerical and managerial processes. Quality circles, and the more recent focus on teamwork both derive from this work. Because of the inherently complex nature of business processes, there's great potential for realigning organization structure and performance measure to satisfy motivators in new ways.

Resources

Conflicts with Motivators

Since humans are typically an organization's most precious resource, there is a direct tie to motivators. Yet facilities, information systems, and technology also need to be in harmony with people's motivators. It's extraordinarily easy for the nonhuman resources to take precedence because they tend to be inherently less flexible, and therefore less tolerant, than humans. Too much of this and you get "sick buildings" where morale has gone down and sick leave has shot up.

Potential Solutions

The trend is to use technology to amplify the skills of humans, rather than try to replace them per se; humans should pace technology rather than the other way around. Facilities should reflect the need for people to interact socially and to satisfy needs that may only be apparent when you understand the unwritten rules by which they operate. Even in environments where managers believe that people's motivators are very simple, they will in reality be *complex* and should be reflected fully.

Organization

Conflicts with Motivators

This is one of the most common sources of conflict with motivators: "The career progression policy forces me to keep job hopping, but I would love to stay put and see my pet project through to fruition. I'm rewarded with bonus payments, but what I find really rewarding is access to exciting new projects, and that's allocated almost randomly. I'm supposed to empower my employees, but I like power myself. We are trying to reorganize into a less bloated firm, but I want my empire."

Potential Solutions

The key to solving these sorts of conflicts is flexibility. Unless your organization is full of clones, it's very undesirable to treat everybody in the same way. Some people can stay in their current roles for longer than usual, and then catch up on the career progression ladder. The reward system can be more imaginative and offer exciting work, training, even pats on the back, but for all of these, you will only know what you need to do if you understand the unwritten rules first.

Shots (big)

Taken together, the real big shots in an organization, the *enablers*, frequently interact with every aspect of the business to make things happen. That's how they come to be enablers in the first place. The bad news is that as a result there's great potential for misalignment at strategic, process, resource, and organizational levels. The good news, though, is experience shows that if you understand the unwritten rules well enough to decode where the misalignment is coming from, you can achieve major realignment in only about one year.

Strategy

Conflicts with Enablers

Stating in the strategy that "quality" or "customer service" or "new product development" is important to your organization, and then giving someone a grandiose title and the responsibility to make it all happen, does not of itself achieve very much. Many senior vice presidents for quality have found themselves isolated from the mainstream and many new product managers have found themselves waging war with the whole of the rest of the business.

Potential Solutions

The generic solution is to give the chosen individual teeth as well as responsibility, but to do so in such a way that conflicts are not forced undercover. The only way to do that is first to understand where possible conflict would come from—by uncovering the unwritten rules. You can then take actions to resolve the potential conflict at the same time as you grant the power for your champion to become a true enabler in the eyes of those in the body of the organization.

Processes

Conflicts with Enablers

In most processes there are—sometimes explicit—sign-offs. These may be at milestones in the process, or else at potential forks in the process where subsequent activities may be very different depending on the decisions made. All too often such sign-off points have been designed for top management to check up with what's going on rather than for the guidance of an empowered workforce. Similarly, many processes remain the province of one function or another, resulting in turf battles.

Potential Solutions

The definitions of milestones and decision points can be totally rewritten so that they provide *guidance* to people. To avoid conflicts with empowerment, the checks and goal posts should be the same ones that people using them would construct if they were conducting the activities as part of their own business. That approach tends to guarantee alignment with top managers as well. Careful use of cross-functional teams can align otherwise conflicting enablers and diminish turf wars.

Resources

Conflicts with Enablers

The two most common reasons companies tend to give as explanations of poor performance are inadequate or inappropriate personnel and lack of skills. Occasionally they're right. Some managers simply may not know how to delegate or think strategically. Some may simply not be willing or capable of truly delegating or thinking strategically. Other resources also often conflict. Information systems are frequently fragmented, and office space reinforces cliques and functional chimneys.

Potential Solutions

If individuals do not know *how* to be appropriate enablers, then train them. But be careful not to confuse this solution with what is needed if there's a conflict with motivators. Training teamwork or empowerment is not a solution if training and delegation are themselves in head-on conflict with what is important to people. If people are unable or unwilling to learn then you may need to replace them. But be *so* careful not to mistake obstinacy with inherent conflict of unwritten rules.

Organization

Conflicts with Enablers

Some resource problems may actually be caused by organizational structure and related systems. Computers may be fragmented because individual functions make the decisions on what to buy, and will resist all attempts from the head office to impose something from above. However, many organizational conflicts with enablers are direct. For instance, "My line boss dictates all my rewards so I'll do nothing to appear disloyal—even if that means I don't work with other functions."

Potential Solutions

Change the organization structure and systems. Rather than impose from headquarters, have a multifunctional group decide the optimal cross-company computer system, reward system, or whatever. Stop local parochialism by having someone other than a line boss specify selected key long-term rewards such as career progression. Maybe adopt a mentor system, in which individuals maintain a sponsor from another part of the business throughout their progress through the organization.

Trigger happy

Triggers are those measures, objectives, or goals that individuals perceive as critical. Vision statements and strategies can act as triggers. Process definitions are full of triggers. Human Resources tends to be managed using triggers. Organizational systems are based around triggers. It's no surprise that triggers are the most frequently changed aspects of business. Maybe, as a result, we've all become so conditioned to quickly interpreting changes in triggers that realignment of triggers often results in a major behavior change in about six months.

Strategy

Conflicts with Triggers

Many company strategists pin their hopes on the ability of employees to act as team players, while all their performance measures are for individuals. Other strategies are so abstract that individuals in the body of the company cannot see what the implications are for them. Several strategies have acted as indicators of what was legitimate research, and have stifled innovative work in other areas. And some strategies have been so unclear that everyone's response was ad hoc.

Potential Solutions

Be wary of the goal of "teams" per se. You may instead want to promote a sense of community in which people are still encouraged to excel as individuals but to do so in a way that promotes a win for themselves and the organization as a whole. Detail strategies so that individuals can use them as performance indicators. Allow inherent flexibility within some aspects of the strategy so that what was designed as a route map to a golden age does not instead end as a gilded prison.

Processes

Conflicts with Triggers

We've already considered the problems of milestones and decision points when related to enablers—they also create conflicts with triggers. Too often the sign-off points are perceived as bureaucratic hurdles imposed by top management. They become key triggers for sanctions, usually perceived as "top management beating us over the head." Errors, generally, are adopted as triggers for blame. As a result, errors are seen as signs of poor performance and so are to be avoided.

Potential Solutions

Milestones should act as triggers for teams doing the work rather than for top managers. Failure to reach a milestone should offer chances to improve the process rather than degenerate into finger pointing. Indeed, errors and failure generally should be sought out rather than hidden. Reporting failure must not result in what feels like a penalty. If you called your dog and then, when she came, screamed at her for being slow, you would not improve matters. Humans are even more sensitive.

Resources

Conflicts with Triggers

Cellular phones, voice mail, and electronic mail are all wonderful in their place, but, my goodness, they can certainly lead to information overload. More and more executives are complaining to me about the time they spend wading through unnecessary messages. What has happened is that the information contained in those messages is perceived by someone as a potential trigger for something. So they pass it on, because it's so easy to do so. If they pass it to you, be flattered. You must be an enabler.

Potential Solutions

Understand why they're passing on the information in the first place. See what perceived reward they are seeking or what penalty they're trying to avoid. Much of the deluge can be people covering their backs. Satisfy their needs in a different way—for example by removing the source of insecurity. Then you can impose filters or discipline into the system. Introducing them earlier will force things undercover. Letting your voice mail fill without checking it, however, is not a solution.

Organization

Conflicts with Triggers

So many personnel policies relate to triggers that it can sometimes prove almost impossible to introduce a change without creating conflict. As we've seen, individuals rather than groups tend to be rewarded directly and indirectly. Failure tends to be punished rather than used as a learning experience. And appraisal systems tend to be designed to encourage everybody to be good at everything, rather than to encourage refinement of individual specialisms.

Potential Solutions

Some organizations are successfully applying team rewards in the form of bonuses or career progression. Contingent compensation systems are being modified to encourage genuine cross-functional cooperation. Some top executives have had their minds concentrated by having up to half their salaries made dependent on *joint* performance.

That's enough generalities. The next two parts of the book are full of specific examples.

Come on, now! We <u>must</u> be able to think of at least one problem that explains our poor corporate performance ...

6
Action
Adventures

The following eight case studies will begin to give you a feel for how you can apply an understanding of the unwritten rules to make changes that free you from barriers to change.

Each section follows the same format:

- *The cause for concern that top managers were facing*
- *The main symptoms that they observed*
- *Additional symptoms*
- *Examples of unwritten rules within the body of the organization*
- *The primary focus of change with regard to modifying the unwritten rules*
- *The main management levers chosen to instigate the change*
- *The approach adopted when implementing the change*
- *The changes made to written rules*
- *The resulting changes in behavior.*

The case studies have been chosen to illustrate the wide variety of solutions that managers adopt. The first four studies examine diverse situations all exhibiting the same main symptoms but requiring very different solutions. The solutions are, primarily, organizational, resource-oriented, process-oriented, and strategic in nature. The next four case studies—exhibiting assorted symptoms—have solutions that follow the same basic sequence as the first four, but with additional contributing factors.

Back to the Future

Cause for Concern

Remember the consumer products company at the beginning of the book? Despite two years of trying to encourage genuine teamwork, cross-functional cooperation, creative risk taking, and long-term thinking throughout the company, little had improved. The overriding cause for concern was the same one that had started the improvement initiative off two years before: how to improve the hit rate of the "right products at the right time." Everyone had turned their backs to the future.

Main Symptoms

What were the main symptoms? Long lead times and poor cooperation—take particular note of these, you'll be seeing them again. Above everything, though, the organization was cynical about the improvement initiative. Now, what is corporate cynicism often the side effect of? It is an initiative that conflicts with an important motivator for many people, but which they can pay lipservice to. Now we're getting somewhere.

Additional Symptoms

Rapid job hopping, parochialism, short-termism, unimaginative products, poor teamwork—were rapidly driving the CEO toward a nervous breakdown, not to mention the loss of his job.

Examples of Unwritten Rules

"We're all ambitious, and here you climb to the top by having breadth rather than depth of experience, so keep job hopping."

"Your line boss can grant accelerated promotion, so keep him or her happy."

"... stand out from the crowd."

"... avoid association with failure."

"You're rewarded primarily for good performance in your own area, so protect your own turf."

"... watch your quarterlies."

Primary Focus of Change

Well, it's the motivators isn't it? It's just as the initial diagnosis predicted. Everyone in the consumer products company is massively ambitious, they want to get to the top of the company, and for that they need to get through as many different jobs in different parts of the company as possible. Big surprise: They're not overly concerned with long-term thinking, cannot run the risk of "being creative" and have little interest in submerging their egos and becoming hidden in a team because they need to stand out to be noticed.

If one of their prime motivators were not career progression then they wouldn't need to behave that way. The rest of the logic would all become redundant. So, the enablers and triggers, although important, are not the primary focus for change.

But, should the CEO try to *change* his people's motivators? Should he tell them not to be so ambitious? No, of course not. Instead, he needs to satisfy the same motivator in a new way.

Primary Levers for Change

Organizational levers: the reward system and the policy for career progression. People often tend to assume that the most natural levers for realigning unwritten rules are organizational, human-resource levers. Our first example will satisfy that predilection; most others will not.

Approach to Change

The CEO identified the inappropriate behaviors encouraged by the existing system and agreed to the behaviors that he wanted and how to encourage them. Then he told key managers of "small modifications" to the career development policy. Very soon after, he relaunched an apparently unrelated awareness and training program designed to encourage genuine cross-functional teamwork, longer-term perspective, consistency of purpose, and overall willingness to change.

Changes to Written Rules

The CEO reduced job hopping by making a deal with his key managers that they would stay in their current jobs for five years instead of job hopping after two or three. But he made sure that he still satisfied the desire for career progression that was actually motivating people, by rewarding their patience with the chance to move *two* rungs up the corporate ladder, rather than just one. So, the motivator remained the same but was satisfied in a new way.

What's more, the new job would not be decided by someone's line boss, who might still be parochial in attitude, but by a mentor in another part of the business. So, the enabler was changed. And that mentor would look for a demonstrated track record of participation in teams that proved creative and willing to think longer term. So, the trigger was also changed. All these changes the CEO reinforced by his own leadership and the example of his top managers.

Resulting Changes in Behavior

Radical changes were evident within six months because the behavior encouraged by the training program was no longer in conflict with people's self interest. They stopped thinking just short-term, because they recognized that they would be staying in their current jobs long enough for medium- to long-term planning to show results. Networking increased as people decided that the payoffs would be tangible and the time spent working for other functions would not appear "disloyal"—at least not to their mentor. In addition, it paid to take some risk.

Star Wars

Cause for Concern

It was the best of times; it was the worst of times. A major international service company was gearing up for the unified market in Europe. Unheard of benefits were promised as a result of the trade barriers coming down between the member states. Yet despite corporate restructuring across Europe in preparation for the unified market, there remained major inefficiencies in internal trading between different national subsidiaries of the company—particularly among the best performing "star subs"—leading to poor service for European customers.

Main Symptoms

Long lead times, poor cooperation. Same as in the last example. In fact, you'll find that the main symptoms of the next two examples are the same as well. And that's very important. Not because the symptoms of long lead times and poor cooperation are themselves special—although they are quite common—but because you'll see that the root causes of all of these first four examples are *totally different*. What's more, the appropriate solutions are totally different as well.

So, it's meaningless to try to create a cookbook of different symptoms and then list the cures appropriate to each symptom. It's only when you uncover the unwritten rules that you can understand what on earth is going on. Exactly the same symptoms may be caused by any number of utterly different reasons. So, a cure that may work perfectly in one organization, may fail totally in your own—even though you exhibit the same symptoms—because it's the wrong cure.

To most competent executives, that's obvious. Yet it's incredible how many management consultants nevertheless still walk into a company, hear about poor lead times or inadequate cross-functional cooperation, and without more ado immediately react by spouting forth on "time-based competition," or "process reengineering," or "strategic realignment" or whatever other panacea they're currently peddling. I wish that they'd explain to the rest of us mere mortals just how they accomplish the superhuman leap of clairvoyant insight they must go through to feel so sure that their pet approach is actually appropriate.

Additional Symptoms

High cost base; frenetic management activity at group level to compensate for lack of accurate and timely information; inability of
headquarters to get all the different subsidiaries to pull together. It
was this latter symptom that was paramount. Headquarters was not
sufficiently key to avoid corporate isolation. That side effect typically
follows from weaker conflicts with important enablers. The danger
was that if HQ pushed too hard it could result in corporate civil war.

Examples of Unwritten Rules

"Push the special needs of your national subsidiary."
"Don't trust head office directives."
"Pay lip service to 'group policy.'"
"Do your own thing."

Primary Focus of Change

Enablers.

Primary Levers for Change

Resource levers—information and information systems.

Approach to Change

Management information systems were out of balance with group
strategy. Fragmented computer systems built around independent
national activities were inhibiting regional-level business planning and
operations. A new approach was needed to integrate Europe-wide
information systems. Instead of trying to drive this from the head
office, foreign subsidiaries were given responsibility for developing
different aspects of the new systems policy. So, the enablers for coming
up with the new system were changed.

Changes to Written Rules

A new European systems policy emerged from the joint activities of
several multinational working parties. The policy specified a single
type of computer hardware and software. Each country adopted the

policy. As a result, the key enabler for access of the right information to the right people at the right time was changed. In this case the enabler is not one or more people—it's a computer system.

Resulting Changes in Behavior

National information systems managers no longer felt threatened by inappropriate head office directives because the managers were themselves now responsible for jointly creating the directives. An atmosphere of constructive cooperation rapidly developed across the European subsidiaries. As a result, Europe-wide systems started to converge. The initial change in behavior was then strongly reinforced as people found that accurate cross-border planning and effective regional operations were now achievable.

This sequence is typical: You encourage people to act in a new way as a means to an end of achieving what is important to them. As they find that the new behavior is valuable in its own right, so the transition is consolidated. Yet the speed of change is far faster than if you only try to encourage people to behave in the new way by attempting to convince them that the behavior is worthwhile in its own right. Try that and they may simply not agree with you.

The Untouchables

Cause for Concern

This was a major heavy-engineering company. They knew all about how to develop and manufacture complex pieces of equipment. Years before they had adopted a "phased review process" to help manage the complex migration of an initial idea dreamed up in an R&D laboratory through prototyping, development, and upscale to a production environment, roll out to the market, tracking in the market place, and finally to eventual withdrawal and replacement by something else. As development and production moved from one phase to another, managers used milestone reviews to check progress.

Yet, despite all of this sophistication, new product development took significantly longer than for leading competitors. Something needed to be done.

Main Symptoms

Long lead times, poor cooperation—once again.

Additional Symptoms

Conflicting objectives, lack of delegation, handover problems between functions, milestones signed off when only partially completed, people playing games with the phased review system. All of this sounds like a cross between corporate power play and corporate camouflage.

Examples of Unwritten Rules

"The milestone reviews are a set of bureaucratic hurdles—so get through them by any means available."

"Expect the other functions to be out for themselves, so fight for the rights of your own function."

"Push for approval for the next phase provided that *most* objectives of the previous phase have been met."

"Tell top management what they want to hear provided it gets them off your back."

"Expect top management to keep moving the goal posts."

Primary Focus of Change

Enablers and triggers. After all, these are what seem to be causing most of the trouble. Conflicting enablers in the different functions are resulting in power struggles close to corporate civil war. All the functions seem like chimneys. None of the departments seem to want to reach out and touch each other. Conflicting triggers mean that everyone is playing games with the milestone reviews, and if things degenerate still further the company runs the risk of moving toward corporate gridlock.

Primary Levers for Change

Process levers. Specifically, the product development and production process.

Approach to Change

The existing milestone review process had been designed for top managers to catch people out, rather than for providing guidance to different functions on what they should do. A multidisciplinary team was set up to redesign the review system to achieve the right balance between control and delegation. They developed a draft manual of generic objectives for each business function for each important phase of product development. They detailed the objectives by including all the questions that project teams would want answers to if the business were their own. They also redefined the role of top management within the review process. The draft manual was then applied on a pilot development project and refined in the light of the experience gained.

Changes to Written Rules

At each review, the completed objectives were to provide management with the information and confidence it needed to authorize the funding and manpower for the next phase. At the review, and only then, management could also refine the development program in the light of outside changes, such as new customer demands or changes in the economy. In the extreme, they could cancel the project—but only once it had reached a milestone. Between phases, a manager's role was not to interfere but to be available as a coach or mentor if needed. So, both enablers and triggers were changed.

Resulting Changes in Behavior

Multidisciplinary product development teams immediately started using the milestone objectives for their own guidance, with each function knowing what input it needed to make at which times. As a result, within months teams found they were able to work faster and in parallel while reducing unnecessary duplication of effort.

To start with, it was not so much that the different functions started to trust each other, but that they felt there were clear performance indicators against which their rivals could be held accountable. Teams stopped being demotivated by the fear of top management diverting, or even canceling, their project in the middle of a phase. They soon began to feel genuinely empowered, and handover problems started to seem like a reflection on the ability and professionalism of the team rather than the selfishness of a given function.

Gradually, as a track record of success developed, the different functions realized the conflicting pressures they had all been under, and then genuinely began to trust each other. Once again, by aligning enablers and triggers with motivators, desired behavior was achieved as a means to an end long before people continued to follow the new behavior because they believed in its merits.

Kustomer Versus Kustomer

Cause for Concern

The Components group of an international computer company sold key electronic components to other divisions of the company as well as to outside customers. But it had a reputation for poor service, both internally and externally. Frustration was building on all sides and the future of the group was becoming uncertain. Nobody knew what the implications for the rest of the company were.

Main Symptoms

Long lead times, poor cooperation. This is the last time. We will look at this final instance of an organization sharing the same main symptoms as the last three cases, before we move onto other examples.

Additional Symptoms

The trouble with all these key components was that they tended to be nonstandard. There was no history of conformance to de facto industry standards. On the contrary, the Components group took the attitude that they were innovative and clever enough to create new standards. Unfortunately, the components were often technologically second-rate, so in practice the world rarely beat a path to their door.

Examples of Unwritten Rules

"When components are in short supply, sell them to the customer that can exert the most pressure—usually an internal division of the company as opposed to an external customer."

"Get new components that can offer competitive advantage out to external customers as fast as possible, and charge them a premium."

"Milk the captive internal market."

"Always get the best deal for the group—unless one of the divisions puts the screws on you."

"There is no right answer, so make up your own rules as you go along."

Primary Focus of Change

At first glance the behavior being exhibited appears to be corporate civil war. But wait a minute. It's not quite as clear cut as that. Yes, there's a lot of battling going on, but who's battling whom? When do you side with which group? There is no consistent answer. Sometimes the Components group is on the side of the divisions, sometimes on the side of the external customers, sometimes fighting for itself—but only when it can get away with it. The real insight comes from the last unwritten rule: "Make up your own rules." That's exactly what's going on—which leads to corporate anarchy. This suggests that something is wrong with the triggers.

Primary Levers for Change

Strategic levers: specifically, the key components and outsourcing strategy itself.

Approach to Change

Many of the unwritten rules were found to have arisen because of the absence of a clear key components strategy or of a comprehensive corporate "make or buy" strategy. The problem was not that people were being bloody minded or belligerent. They simply were not provided with any clear guidance on how to resolve the inherent tradeoffs between the various interested parties.

Top management from across the company and from key external customers evaluated the conflicts in trying to satisfy each of the stakeholders in the Components group: internal customers, external customers, employees, and owners. Having listed each of their needs, they realized for the first time just how much in conflict some of them were. Far too much opposed, in fact, to expect managers of the components group to decide issues consistently on an ad hoc basis.

So, in an off-site workshop, representatives of each of the main stakeholders worked through the tradeoffs one by one and agreed on mutually acceptable ways to resolve the conflicts.

Changes to Written Rules

The agreement was published in the form of an explicit key components charter, including:

When components are in short supply they should be _spread_ //
proportionally across _all_ outstanding orders.   ..

New components that could offer competitive advantage to   ✓
internal customers should be withheld from external
customers for six months.

Internal customers are no longer captive but instead can   YES
purchase externally.

Resulting Changes in Behavior

Frustration of both internal and external customers dropped as soon as they realized that they could expect a fair crack at the whip. Internal customers started working closely with the Components group to develop competitive products to which they knew they would get six months exclusive rights. Meanwhile, the components group quickly saw which way the wind was blowing and became highly responsive to internal customers—knowing that otherwise their previously captive customers could go elsewhere. Gradually, this led to far more competitive products that were on the cutting edge of the industry. The world started to beat a path to their door after all.

Leave and Let Die

Cause for Concern

A chemicals company had a number of processing plants, some of them handling highly dangerous substances. It was understandably very concerned about potential accidents that might cause hazards to the health of its employees as well as potential damage to the environment. It regularly conducted environmental health and safety audits and monitored the performance of its plants using a variety of measures.

Two of the measures common to the industry are reported incidents and accidents. An *incident* is when someone trips over a badly shut access hatch, recovers her balance, and walks on. An *accident* is when another person trips over the same hatch, twists an ankle, and spills the sample of flammable solvent she was carrying. An incident is an accident waiting to happen. For a given type of plant, the number of reported incidents and accidents can often be predicted.

But there was a problem: At one of the company's best plants, although the number of reported incidents remained at normal levels, the number of accidents was gradually creeping upward. To most people working on the site the progression was imperceptible. But to the safety officer, the graph on his office wall was becoming a concern. He waited a few weeks, and it kept climbing. He showed it to the site manager. They decided that they needed to do something practical.

Main Symptoms

Increasing minor accidents. Normal levels of reported incidents.

Additional Symptoms

None. The site had an excellent record. Morale and commitment were very high. That was what was so confusing. So, they decided to analyze the unwritten rules and find out just what was going on.

Examples of Unwritten Rules

"Be a member of the team."

"Be seen as professional by your peers and your boss."

"All pull together—always help out a colleague because it might be the other way around next time."

"Don't get hung up with the 'letter of the law'—do what's necessary for the smooth running of the site whatever it may say in your job description."

Primary Focus of Change

What was going on? The exemplary set of unwritten rules was actually fighting the very behavior that everyone wanted. If Bill tripped over an access hatch that Sam should have shut properly, then Bill closed the hatch on Sam's behalf. Of course Bill would not report such a minor incident because that would be like stabbing Sam in the back. It would seem like pointing the finger at lack of professionalism, and in no way is Sam unprofessional. Anyway, Sam would do exactly the same thing if roles were reversed. Bill will mention it to Sam, which will be just as good as preventing the same thing from happening again, and a lot less public.

The trouble is, it's *not* just as good. The reason that Sam did not close the hatch properly was not that she forgot. She did close it. But the catch is worn and after a few hours, if the pump above it is at full speed, the vibration works the catch open. It will do so again later when Peter is on shift but it will not be reported. It will slip open again when Paul takes over, but again no one will report it. It will come unshut once more, just in time for Mary to trip over while carrying her flammable solvent. There's no problem, provided that any sparking from the electrical pump motor has been reported as an incident earlier and so repaired ...

Of all things, what we have here is corporate rebellion. People were choosing not to respond to the trigger to report incidents. And they were doing it not because they were rebellious, but because they were so nice. Because they were not reporting minor incidents, they were inadvertently preventing any possibility of highlighting potential causes of accidents. So, as plant machinery became worn and equipment developed intermittent faults, so eventually the number of accidents derived from the unreported incidents crept up.

Primary Levers for Change

Organizational, with aspects of process.

Approach to Change

The problem may have been worrying and insidious. The root cause may have been deceptive. We may only have discovered what was going on by tracking back through a convoluted route of logic. But whoever said that the solution had to be equally complicated?

It turned out to be the simplest thing in the world. The site manager simply pointed out to everyone what was going on. He reminded them that the most supportive way that they could help their colleagues was potentially to save their lives. Everybody already knew the rest.

Changes to Written Rules

None. By his actions and behavior, the site manager reinforced the existing policies. He reassured everybody that they should interpret reported incidents as positive attempts to prevent accidents, rather than negative bureaucracy to record errors that had already been corrected.

Resulting Changes in Behavior

Within two weeks the ratio of reported incidents to accidents improved dramatically. For a while the absolute number of reported incidents was higher than on comparable sites. Then the number of accidents dropped to *below* the average on other sites. Everything was back on course.

A Depot Too Far

Cause for Concern

A large office consumables company had thousands of products on its catalogue. Despite this large number, the company presented a single face to the customer: offering one-stop shopping for all the items. But sometimes customers would call and ask about the status of a shipment they had already ordered. Or they would ask to change one item in the order: "Can we change blue-white paper to off-white? It's the same price in the catalogue, so it doesn't make any difference overall."

And that caused havoc. Although the computer would come back with a reply, all too often it was wrong. "Your order is on the road," should have been, "It's held up waiting for one of the stock items. Do you want it delivered now or shall we wait until it's complete?" "I've changed the blue-white to off-white," should have been, "Unfortunately, the shipment with your original blue-white order is already on its way to you. I'll tell the driver to separate it from the delivery to you this afternoon and I'll send the replacement off-white to you straight away."

Main Symptoms

Inaccurate deliveries, broken promises to customers.

Additional Symptoms

Building frustration from the Customer Service Department.

Now, wait a moment, what has this got to do with the unwritten rules? It all seems pretty straightforward. In one form or another it's a logistics and distribution problem. Maybe the computer systems are not sophisticated enough to track what's going on. Maybe there's insufficient communication throughout the distribution network, so drivers can't be contacted when en route. Maybe the warehousing should be rationalized to make it easier to change orders. But one thing is perfectly clear: This is not an unwritten rules of the game problem.

Or is it? Usually, we use the rule of thumb that if a problem is prefixed by "What" then it does not directly need rules of the game analysis to solve it. So, "What markets should we be addressing?" or "What technology will become dominant over the next decade?" do not require that you understand unwritten rules. However, when you ask "How" or "Why" then things change. "How can we integrate the new technology?" or "Why did we never see that there was an ideal market under our noses?" may both have heavy unwritten rules components.

To decide the kind of problem the office consumables company was facing, we have to ask a standard question: *Why, if the organization is full of competent people, did this ever arise in the first place?* So, we have to consider why a firm that so clearly understood the importance of customer service and had done so much to automate its operations, nevertheless let such major logistics and distribution problems develop.

Examples of Unwritten Rules

"As a warehouse manager you have as much freedom as you can make for yourself—so carve yourself a niche."

"Stay out of the clutches of the head office."

"Small is beautiful because no one can see you—so manage the growth of your empire so that it's big enough but not *too* big."

"The warehouse managers can do favors for those of us in head office when we get in a bind—so don't rub them the wrong way."

"The warehouses can cause real problems if they're not on your side because there are strong personalities involved—so divide and conquer."

Primary Focus of Change

Now does it make a bit more sense? The problems in distribution and warehousing were not coincidental, they were systemic. The problems had periodically been addressed in the past, but nothing tangible had happened. There were still about 30 warehouses spread over only a few hundred square miles. And everybody involved at the warehouse level wanted it that way. Deep down, everybody involved at the head office level wanted it that way as well. In essence, everyone was subverting attempts to change because no one really wanted to change.

If merely the symptom of the problem were addressed—the inefficient warehousing system—then either the solution would never get implemented or else similar problems would spring up in the future.

Instead, they needed to address the root cause. Corporate subversion suggests conflicts with motivators. So that was the focus of change.

Primary Levers for Change

What we assumed from the start: resource and process levers, in the form of warehousing and the distribution and logistics process.

Approach to Change

The company decided to bite the bullet once and for all. They knew that there was an irreconcilable mismatch between the motivators that they wanted for their warehouse managers and what they actually had. They could see no way to satisfy the old motivators in a new way. This was not going to be one of the painless rules of the game solutions.

Changes to Written Rules

The whole distribution network was heavily rationalized to a few sites. Few of the original warehouse managers chose to remain and they were not encouraged to stay. A new generation emerged from the ranks.

Resulting Changes in Behavior

The vicious spiral was broken forever. Warehouse managers no longer had the empires or personalities that were the root of the puzzle. It had never been just a logistics problem. It was a people problem all along.

Robocop

Cause for Concern

A manufacturer that was supplier to the top tier of the automotive industry was always under strong pressure to be responsive to the whims of customers. In the mid 1980s the firm introduced high levels of flexible automation to its shop floor—primarily in the form of industrial robots and computer numerical control lathes and milling machines.

But the company kept hitting problems. Despite high levels of automation, it proved impossible to make rapid changes in designs. Silly oversights led to disproportionate disruption. Mistakes, which were obvious with 20/20 hindsight, remained uncorrected until they caused major problems much later. And yet it appeared to be nobody's fault. Managers and supervisors took their work very seriously, and the workforce were friendly and did everything that was asked of them. Yet still the company hit problems.

Main Symptoms

Inability to make rapid design changes in response to customer requests.

Additional Symptoms

High maintenance costs.

What's actually going on down on the shop floor?

Examples of Unwritten Rules

"Do what you're told."

"The robots provide the brains—so check yours in at the factory gate."

"Initiative is neither rewarded nor wanted—so keep your head down and keep your mouth shut."

"We're a friendly bunch on the shop floor, and nobody likes you if you cause waves—so try to agree with everyone."

Primary Focus of Change

Those unwritten rules are bad news. It's not that the workforce is actively sabotaging the shop floor, but they have turned off. It's an early form of corporate suicide. The automation has been introduced in such a way that the remaining workforce has been left subservient and demotivated. All their motivators, other than money and a job, have been disregarded. Of course they don't show initiative. Of course they don't pipe up with suggestions of better ways to do things or to avoid problems. Of course they don't offer short cuts. Why should they? All opportunities for them to act as human resources to the company have systematically been cut off. They are the worst side effect of the "scientific Taylorism" that started in the 1920s. Their humanity has been degraded to the level of machine. When one of the machine supervisors was asked why he had never passed on a tip that subsequently saved the company a small fortune in maintenance costs, he replied: "Because the S.O.B.s never asked me before ..."

Primary Levers for Change

Unlike the previous example, in this case it was not only possible to satisfy the motivators of the shop floor workers in a new way—it was also highly desirable. Without doing so, the company would have been operating with one hand behind its back. It was paying its workforce the going rate for human beings, but then using only a fraction of their brainpower. That's a luxury that may have made economic sense when humans did not cost very much to abuse. But these days few companies can afford it. To correct the trend of corporate suicide, the firm needed to redress the balance of process, resource, and organizational levers.

Approach to Change

First, the company had to stem the tide of cold application of sterile computers and frigid robots that, as in all too many other organizations, was stifling the creativity of the human workforce.

Don't get me wrong, I love computing and robotics. No, really. I have an honors degree in one and a Ph.D. in the other, and my first book was devoted to the joys of applying both. The technologies themselves are wonderfully exciting and massively life enhancing. But exactly those same technologies can be woefully misapplied and cause degradation and demotivation and create unintended negative side effects so great that they can build to corporate suicide.

The second aspect of the approach was to involve the workforce in working with experts in flexible manufacturing system (FMS) technology to develop systems that would act more as amplifiers of skills the workforce already had, or could be trained to have, rather than as replacements and alternatives to those human skills. So, for example, a craftsman was trained to evaluate complex, expensive but delicate machined parts. Based on his own judgment, he could then select which of a variety of further machining operations were needed to complete the part in the minimum number of operations.

Changes to Written Rules

Every new system specification was designed to maximize leverage of human skill and judgment. In addition, modifications to existing FMS units were gradually introduced. The pay system was changed to encourage workers to broaden their skills, and training was offered as a reward for work well done and initiative taken. A suggestion box was introduced, with bonuses and training offered for good ideas.

Resulting Changes in Behavior

Over the following year, the whole attitude of the workforce changed. They were the same people (indeed, turnover on the shop floor dropped dramatically), but the workers started to contribute. They began to catch errors before they occurred. They took short cuts. They made the organization responsive. They pulled their company back from the brink.

Honey, I Downsized
the Business

Cause for Concern

In the early 1990s, the R&D division of one of the large multinationals
went through a major downsizing. Like many others, they decided that
it was no longer a tenable strategy to conduct basic research. Indeed,
economic pressures convinced them that nearly all their R&D should
actually be applied development with a likely gestation period of only
a couple of years. And they should do no genuine research at all.

This decision was forced through, despite strenuous opposition
from the head of the division who subsequently resigned. Then the
axe began to swing. In each wave of cuts, hundreds of people lost their
jobs. Morale hit its lowest point. Then the cuts stopped. A memo
announced that the worst was over and that the challenge now was to
build a new organization on the foundation that remained. A strategy
statement was circulated. Everyone held their breath. Would it work?

Main Symptoms

Shell shock. After 18 months of downsizing, everyone felt like they
had survived a series of terrorist bombing raids. Nothing would ever
be the same again. All bets were off. What would happen now?

Additional Symptoms

There were positive signs that people had realigned themselves to the
needs of the business units. A staff survey showed that morale had
picked up: people talked of "dawn after a long, cold night." The cuts
had felt very painful, and now those who remained could hardly
believe their luck. Everyone desperately wanted to believe that the
organization had made the transition and refocused onto medium-
term market-led demands. But it seemed too good to be true; too rapid
to be sustainable.

Top managers' instinct was to wait though. Do nothing to disrupt
things further. Allow for a period of consolidation. In a year's time,

they could take any corrective action. But just in case, they decided to look at the unwritten rules of their new game first—and *then* wait.

Examples of Unwritten Rules

"The business units now call all the shots—so make sure they value your work by performing well according to the new performance measures."

"The old heady days of high research are gone for good—so concentrate instead on applying your expertise so that it's of practical benefit."

"The company has broken any moral contract for a career within the division—so keep your eyes open for a better job outside the company."

"Your job is only as secure as the renewal of the annual budget of your laboratory—so don't rely on anything more than a year out."

Primary Focus of Change

Report card: good marks for the present, bad marks for the future. Everyone who remained had genuinely come to realize that their future lay with satisfying the business units. They were not paying lipservice. Morale really was picking up. So the current state of the division after downsizing appeared pretty well what the top management had wanted.

But let the model roll forward two years. Everyone had worked out a personal equation of what conditions needed to be satisfied for them to jump ship and join another company—or go independent. When the job market picked up in a couple of years, all the best people would leave because salaries tended to be better outside. In the past this had been countered by job security, but that didn't apply any more. As there were no poor performers left because of the downsizing, the only people left in the division after the cream left would be mediocre. Worse, even within that band of mediocrity, there would be some that had more generalist skills and so be more marketable. They would leave too. So the only people remaining would have a profile of narrow, mediocre specialist. Not exactly the ideal foundation for the new R&D strategy.

And that was the other problem. The strategy required that over the next few years whole laboratories would voluntarily "retread" and learn new development skills. But no one in practice would ever take the risk of deliberately suboptimizing in the short term in order to be in a better position a few years out. It required teams to appear less efficient than they really were, because one or more of them were being trained in new skills. And no team felt secure enough to do that and risk having their budget cut at the year end because they had not been sufficiently productive. The organization was drifting toward corporate panic.

Primary Levers for Change
Strategic and organizational.

Approach to Change
Detail the strategy and become more proactive about keeping people with the appropriate skills and attitudes needed for the strategy to work.

Changes to Written Rules
The R&D strategy was clarified and communicated in sufficient detail that each laboratory could see the implications to themselves. Agreements were reached with each laboratory about when they should retread, and how much their performance might suffer in the process. The most important people for the strategy were approached individually and reassured about how especially valuable they were considered to be.

Resulting Changes in Behavior
The deer dragged their eyes away from the oncoming headlights and started to run. The laboratories moved from the verge of panic to a sense of excitement. The best people became fired up and began to lose interest in leaving. By the time the job market picked up, people felt part of a new type of R&D division. The rebirth had begun in earnest.

By now you should have a feel for the ways that a variety of companies have applied an understanding of the unwritten rules to break free from their stranglehold. Each situation is necessarily unique. Therefore, each solution is necessarily unique as well. That is, after all, the whole point of understanding the unwritten rules in the first place. It's also the reason that there can never be truly off-the-shelf solutions.

But it is possible to recognize some patterns in the most damaging problems caused by unwritten rules. And it is possible to recommend broad approaches to addressing those problems.

The five chapters in the next part of the book follow the same structure as the ones you've just read, namely: cause for concern, main symptoms, additional symptoms, and so on. But they're not case studies of specific companies. Rather they are generic composites built up from a variety of companies. They address five of the most prevalent yet damaging side effects in organizations today: isolated and ineffective top management; untapped potential from failed change initiatives; institutionalized discrimination; failed mergers, acquisitions, and joint ventures; and companies that lose their way and become dinosaurs.

Each of these side effects can be prevented if only you use the unwritten rules to understand what is going on. Happy reading ...

And the vacation in Hawaii, for the <u>individual</u> who stood out as being the best <u>team</u> player, goes to ...

7
Twentieth-Century Flops

Silence
of the Lambs

Cause for Concern

So many CEOs that I talk with are feeling isolated. Others don't feel isolated. But they are. Sometimes, the whole of the top management are out of touch with what is really going on in the body of their organizations. They have become an elite.

A few years ago I was working for an international company that throughout its long history had been a household name. The directorate was filled with the great and the good and operated like an exclusive club. Over several months I became friendly with one of the directors. One evening, after several glasses of wine, he regaled me with the story of how he had first heard that he had been promoted to his directorship. One of the existing directors had sent him a telegram. Hoping that it was good news, my friend had torn open the envelope. There were only four words: "Welcome to Corporate Heaven."

Less than a year after I heard this story, the president of the same corporation was reported in national newspapers making statements about his company that were subsequently shown to be so out of touch with reality that he lost all credibility. He was publicly humiliated and pilloried by the press. Yet still he could not understand how he could have been so out of touch. He had been caught completely unawares. Within a week he was forced to resign.

The trouble is, he just happens to be one of the ones who have been caught out. There are many other CEOs that are currently in exactly the same exalted position that he was in just before his fall. They and their executive teams are just as isolated, just as cut off as he was. And they currently feel just as comfortable, just as secure, just as sure of themselves.

Main Symptoms

Elitism. Comfort at the top. The hotel industry is suffering at the moment, yet the top executives of one of the leading chains meet four days out of five in an exclusive dining room and talk about … anything they like. One day a week, they finish work after lunch. They're in no way the only executives to maintain such an incongruous lifestyle.

Additional Symptoms

Smugness. A few months ago I gave a dinner speech on the unwritten rules. Afterwards, the president of a very large company commented to the assembled multitude that although he recognized that unwritten rules existed, he was not sure that he needed to know what they were. A little while later I met with a group of his managers, a few levels down the organization. They had no doubt about the damage that unwritten rules could cause. Subsequently, I went to one of the outposts of their corporate empire. The unwritten rules were wreaking havoc.

Examples of Unwritten Rules

"Be a member in good standing of the corporate club."

"Don't rock the boat."

"Don't tell the president bad news—she shoots the messenger."

"Take advantage of time with the CEO to tell him all the good things you've accomplished since last you met."

Primary Focus of Change

Motivators, enablers, and triggers. There tends to be strong multiple reinforcement of the old behavior. You must break all the causal loops.

Primary Levers for Change

Mainly organizational, with some process changes.

Approach to Change

CEOs have to have the guts to hold a mirror up to themselves and their top management. And then look at the reflection. And then do something about it if they don't like what they see. No, you should not wait until the company is in difficulties before trying to do something. You should not work on the theory that as the executives feel the problems of the company grow, they will be more likely to change their behavior. That is a dangerous myth. Far from making it easier to instigate change at the top, a company moving toward a precipice often finds its executives clinging more strongly to the past. They start to seek the Holy Grail that saved them during the golden age. People are far more open to change when they see the logic behind it. But they also need to feel secure enough to countenance accepting that logic.

Changes to Written Rules

That will depend more on your starting point than where you want to end up. You are aiming for a change in attitudes of those below the top management, as much as a change in behavior of the upper echelon itself. I used to believe that that could not be forced. If messengers always got shot in the past, it's going to take people a long time to be convinced that open season has ended for good. "Yes, Brad. I agree with you. We should tell the president. Go do it!"

Resulting Changes in Behavior

I now realize that you can accelerate the process of acceptance, erasing cynicism, and rebuilding trust. But you need to be open and honest about it and admit any errors of the past. I know of no other approach that works. If you try to keep up a facade and simply change top management behavior, it takes a long time for benefits to accrue. First, people need to notice what you are doing. Next, they have to watch your track record—only then are they convinced. Meanwhile, you have no positive reinforcement for your change, so you will probably slip back to your old ways. Instead, be up-front about what you're doing. It's amazing how supportive people can rapidly become when you tell them what you're committing to. It's similar to giving up smoking.

The Great Change Robbery

Cause for Concern

At the start of this book, I mentioned the apparently increasing rate of failure that top managers feel they are experiencing. They instigate TQM, downsizing, process reengineering, yet feel they get nothing like the full benefits from implementation that they expected. Of course, part of the problem is that the low hanging fruit has already been picked. You have to stretch further to reach the next level of performance improvement opportunities. It's the *dilemma of change* again: The greatest potential improvements come from the approaches that carry the greatest chances of failure.

And the other part of the problem is the human factors involved. As discussed before, each new wave of management techniques requires that you change the ways that people behave. And for reasons that are now hopefully burnt into your subconscious, changing people's behavior can be a real problem if you don't understand the unwritten rules. So that has proven another reinforcement of the likelihood of failure.

The net result of all this is that there is an increasing number of "failed" change initiatives out there that in reality are masking largely untapped benefits. It's not that the potential benefits are not there—managers have done nearly all the right things—but that the few aspects that they have done wrong or missed out completely have created a logjam. The frustration is not that they were unable to reach the high hanging fruit—their fingertips did reach it—they just couldn't get a firm enough grip to pluck it off the branch.

Main Symptoms

Failure to achieve the full benefits of successful implementation.

Additional Symptoms

It may be that people do not really feel too bad about the failure, or maybe do not even perceive the initiative as having become a failure.

Examples of Unwritten Rules

The barriers to change may be caused by any of the types of unwritten rules and unintended negative side effects highlighted throughout this book. But be warned. You need to consider not just the rules that may be creating unintended conflicts with the new process design that you are trying to implement, you also need to consider how they may be creating *barriers to the process of redesigning itself*. In other words, unwritten rules may destroy your chances of successfully reaching the optimum goal because they corrupt the selection of the goal itself.

For example: "Don't waste too much effort on the latest flavor of the month," or "Try to keep everyone happy," or "Only act on consensus," or "Focus only on your own turf," or "Don't encroach on anyone else's turf," or "Don't rock the boat," or "Don't set yourself up for failure by committing to ambitious deliverables," or "Don't be seen to be a radical," or "Don't do anything to design away your own job."

Primary Focus of Change

The whole integrated set of motivators, enablers, and triggers. You cannot do less than address every major unwritten rule related to process selection and design as well as implementation.

Primary Levers for Change

Aligning resources and organization with process.

Approach to Change

There are certain approaches that ought by now to be considered "best practice." First and foremost, involve on the design team people who are going to have to implement the recommendations. Ensure that they all buy into the recommendations. If you involve external experts, insist that they act as coaches to the internal team. Do not delegate responsibility to the outsiders and let them tell the team what the best solution is. Make them help the team figure out for themselves what the solution is. It may not be the same as the academically neat version that the outsiders would come up with alone. Good. That's the whole point.

Ensure ongoing communication between those involved in design and in implementation. Ideally there would be a seamless transition. In practice, at least some people involved will be different. Also, even if a team has been granted authority to come up with plans and implement them, in practice the plans tend to be sufficiently different from the terms of reference that the team started with, that there is usually a digestion period during which a larger group has to be involved.

Finally, do not focus exclusively on coming up with an optimal solution—whether it be for reengineering, quality, or core competencies. Don't even focus exclusively on ensuring implementation of an optimal solution. Focus instead on ensuring a continuous stream of business benefits. Ultimately, that is the only performance measure of any worth.

Changes to Written Rules

More than ever, in this case, changes to the written rules may take the form of top management actions and behavior rather than formalized policies and procedures. Support at the top for the change needs to be communicated by deeds rather than words. This *is* the time for vision and leadership, but display it in the right form. Convey a sense of focus and urgency, but temper it with understanding and knowledge. Provide constructive support, and have the courage to continue that support. But above all, be sensitive to the unwritten rules of your game.

Resulting Changes in Behavior

Only then will the logjam break to release a stream of untapped potential.

She Who Dares Loses

Cause for Concern

Two years ago I was working late with a large multinational corporation. It was 10:30 in the evening. No one had eaten, but I hadn't even mentioned the word "food." Anyone who knows me will recognize this as a clear sign that it must have been a very important meeting indeed.

A director of Human Resources had just completed one of the most spectacularly colorful flip chart diagrams I had ever seen. We all surreptitiously glanced at our watches. "So, have we covered everything?" he asked. His stomach let out a rumble that echoed around the board room.

"Well, there is still the issue of diversity," I offered tentatively.

"Oh yes, I'd left that." His face took on a caring-and-professional-but-really-wants-to-go-home expression. "I'm not sure that that's really a problem here, is it?" He looked hopefully around the rest of the room.

Here we go, I thought. "Well actually," I replied, "you're one of the most racist and sexist organizations I've ever worked with ..."

Main Symptoms

Lack of diversity.

Additional Symptoms

Lack of recognition that there's anything wrong. Intolerance.

Examples of Unwritten Rules

"Fit the right profile."

"Only have a baby after you become successful."

"Don't try to get promoted through the 'glass ceiling.'"

"Don't force your private beliefs on others."

"If you're one of them then you're not one of us."

"Women can't get ahead."

"Blacks can't get ahead."

"Gays can't get ahead."

"Jews can't get ahead."

"If you don't fit in—then get out."

Primary Focus of Change

Understanding how the unwritten rules are reinforcing the lack of diversity and what negative side effects they may have on performance.

Primary Levers for Change

Mainly organizational but with impacts for processes, resources, and balance of stakeholder needs.

Approach to Change

A CEO I know very well said recently that he was not sure that he believed in diversity. He was only interested in how good people were at their jobs, and did not care about race, gender, religion, or sexual orientation. Most people, thank goodness, would these days agree.

Civilized companies recognize that they're shooting themselves in the foot if they consistently undervalue and underutilize sections of their workforce. Indeed, so called "minorities," when taken collectively, often constitute the majority of employees. And sophisticated managers are starting to realize that diversity brings benefits. They find female managers often far better at empathy and at avoiding chronic macho posturing than some of their male colleagues. They find that lesbians and gay men sometimes have greater flexibility and willingness to move locations than colleagues with families. Cultural and ethnic diversity brings new and stimulating perspectives to old problems. And they see skin color as carrying the same relevance as hair color.

But it's not quite so simple. When you analyze the unwritten rules of organizations that have a history of discrimination, you find extraordinarily convoluted reinforcement for the old behavior. Long after the ostensive bigotry is over an insidious echo lingers, often in triggers relating to recruitment policies and evaluation programs. "You would be expected to entertain a great deal so it really helps to have a wife." Try working out just how many narrow minded preconceptions there are in that simple statement. And let's not kid ourselves. I said that the unwritten rules tend to continue working against minorities in organizations with a history of discrimination. There is not a large organization on this planet that does not have a history of discrimination.

Changes to Written Rules

These days we all want teams. But the whole point is that for a team to be optimal it needs diversity. The ideal team composition is not a collection of clones. But the most natural way for a team to compose itself is to invite like minded individuals to become team members.

Part of the solution to all this comes from awareness: training in the benefits of diversity, education about the similarities of the diverse. But then you must address the pernicious causal loops that will continue to fight against that training. Track back to the root of the disease. Unearth the written rules and top management actions that unwittingly are stifling elements of the most precious resource your organization has. Expose what are the most hypocritical, unfair, and unnecessary afflictions to asphyxiate business performance and cut them out.

Resulting Changes in Behavior

If I could wave a magic wand I would wish that this type of change above all others could be fast. But we are touching on key motivators, which are often reinforced by several interrelated triggers and enablers. We may be trying to change what, maybe through ignorance, people sincerely believe. And changing such personal beliefs often takes time.

So, go to it. All the more reason to start doing something now.

Predator

Cause for Concern

One of the largest publishing houses has acquired vast numbers of smaller companies over the years, yet it's extremely difficult for them to work as a coherent whole. Quite separately, a major utility has bought up a number of electrical power generation and distribution companies, but it has been unable to create a unified corporation out of the collection of apparently similar acquisitions.

On a different continent, a large airline has merged with another. Despite good will on both sides, and apparently similar values and beliefs, they are finding it extraordinarily difficult to achieve the full benefits that both sides anticipated from the merger. About the same time, an oil corporation three thousand miles away set up a strategic alliance with a local competitor. Like the airline, they cannot understand why things are not working as well as they should.

And finally, at the turn of the decade a financial institution analyzed the investment potential of a proposed acquisition. On paper everything looked very appealing and they went ahead. Three years later, they have pulled out of the deal. It just hasn't worked. They ended up losing money and no one understood why. The deal still looks good on paper. The concern is, what if a similar deal comes along tomorrow? Should they take it?

Main Symptoms

All the talk about synergy that is prevalent before the acquisition, merger, or alliance, evaporates soon after the deal is struck.

Additional Symptoms

Financial misperformance. Inability to cooperate. Parochialism. Poor communication. Frustration.

Examples of Unwritten Rules

The key insight here is that the actual sets of unwritten rules themselves are not all that critical. It's the *mismatch* of the sets of rules that causes problems. When you analyze the unwritten rules of two organizations as they coalesce, typically you find one of three patterns. If one party is dominant, for instance in an acquisition, then the dominant organization superimposes its key enablers and triggers onto the other organization—usually in the form of transferred key individuals together with corporate wide performance measures and appraisal systems. If, on the other hand, neither party chooses to be dominant, say in a merger or strategic alliance, then one of two things happens. Either both parties try to broadly maintain their existing enablers and triggers, or else they create a new common set that is a genuine derivative from both.

Primary Focus of Change

So, what has happened? In each case, the acquisition, merger, or alliance has deliberately set up the very conditions that tend to occur unintentionally when a major new change initiative is introduced into a company. Namely, new written rules and management actions have been enacted that are likely in conflict with all the existing unwritten rules. In a conventional change initiative, these conflicts are usually a by-product of the change itself. In an acquisition, however, the new written rules are deliberately transplanted, usually *because* they are different from those that were there originally.

Primary Levers for Change

As with any surgical transplant, the donor organ needs to be matched with the recipient or it will be rejected. The new key enablers, triggers, and most certainly any new motivators, all need to be compatible with the existing underlying unwritten rules. But those unwritten rules will still broadly correspond to the *original* motivators, enablers, and triggers from which they were derived. If they are incompatible, you risk a whole spectrum of unintended side effects.

Approach to Change

When a dominant party imposes its own set of management controls on an acquired company, there are bound to be side effects. When two parties broadly try to keep their own controls, then they both suffer because they remain inherently incompatible with each other. Even if both parties are ever so civilized about a merger or alliance, and go to the trouble of creating a new set of joint controls, they still hit problems. Both parties suffer from side effects caused by incompatibility with their original unwritten rules. Now you can see why acquisitions, mergers, and alliances have consistently proven so problematic, and why you cannot decide on the attractiveness of a deal by looking only at financial performance. Instead, you need to carefully align new strategy, processes, resources, and organization with the existing stakeholder needs, original process descriptions, previous resources, and any former organization policies and procedures that you have not yet replaced.

Changes to Written Rules

The only way to see what is needed is to conduct a series of unwritten rules appraisals. Analyze both companies, ideally before imposing any new management systems. Agree before hand what both parties see as the key success factors for the acquisition, merger, or alliance. Those are your starting point. Then conduct appraisals to highlight potential barriers caused by unwritten rules to satisfying those success factors.

Resulting Changes in Behavior

If you conduct the appraisals before the acquisition, merger, or alliance, then hopefully you simply avoid unintended side effects that you will never actually experience. If you're picking up the pieces afterwards, then manage the transition as if you were introducing a change initiative.

Deathwish

Cause for Concern

Some organizations are killing themselves and they don't know it. Corporations that believe they are in a blissful state of supremacy are slipping into a blissful sleep from which they will never awake. Companies are volunteering themselves as examples of excellence at the same time they are volunteering for euthanasia.

Over the last decade, some of the leading bastions of industry in the United States and Europe have horrified onlookers by starting to creak and groan. Solid institutions of unimpeachable standing have begun to slide and realize that in reality they were built on foundations of sand. One-time blue chip companies like Big Blue IBM itself are now being referred to as dinosaurs.

Suddenly no one feels safe any more. Nobody appears immune. Even Asian Pacific corporations are starting to worry. Relatively young companies like Apple Computer agonize that they too may be going the way of the dinosaurs. Smaller companies too are finding themselves caught out by unexpected changes in their markets. As we approach a new millennium, there's an unspoken question on every CEO's mind:

"What should I be doing to ensure that my organization gets through intact?"

Main Symptoms

That's the problem. Nobody knows. Only after the event does everyone start pointing out all the flaws that are obvious with hindsight.

Additional Symptoms

The trite answers tend to be bad strategy and poor management. The common denominator of all the creaking giants—and the creaking dwarfs—is that they did not get their strategies right. Otherwise, by definition of a good strategy, they would have been able to maintain their positions in the market place. And if they didn't have good strategies then, so their critics would maintain, their management must have been poor.

Examples of Unwritten Rules

But that answer simply isn't good enough. It fails the test of every good Rulebuster: "Unless everybody in the organization was incompetent, why did it ever happen?" The point is that claiming that a corporation didn't have as good a strategy as it could have had is not a sufficient explanation as to why it went under. It just sets off an increasingly puzzling dialog:

Q "So why didn't people come up with a better strategy?"
A "Oh, because they had incompetent strategists."
Q "And the CEO didn't realize?"
A "No, he was incompetent."
Q "But why didn't the marketing people point out the shortfall?"
A "Ah, because they didn't have their finger on the pulse of the industry."
Q "Why not?"
A "Because they didn't listen to their customers?"
Q "Because they were incompetent?"
A "That's right!"
Q "And what about the people in R&D? Why didn't they blow the whistle? Were they incompetent also?"
A "No! That was a problem of communication. It was the same with the guys in production. The different functions just didn't talk to each other."
Q "But in that case, why didn't anybody do something about the fact that none of the functions were cooperating with each other?"
A "Ah, well that *was* because they were all incompetent!"

Primary Focus of Change

We need to track back to what is really going on. We need to understand why the organization is locked in a vicious spiral. We need to understand the causal loops encapsulated by the unwritten rules that create the inexorable inevitability that the strategy will be off course.

Primary Levers for Change

Not strategic to start with. That's the end goal. First realign processes, resources, and organization to optimally satisfy all stakeholder needs.

Approach to Change

This is the most complex application I know of the unwritten rules approach. By definition, your whole organization is blinkered to what is going on. You interpret everything with a mindset from the past. You need a real paradigm shift if you are to see things differently. It's not the implementation of your strategy and change programs that you need to address first; it's the forces that affect the construction of the strategy and the change programs themselves that is the focus. You are touching on the very core of your organization's identity. You will almost certainly need some outside help to act as a reality check and sounding board. Remember, you are like a company on a corporate LSD trip—you need someone whom you trust to talk you down.

Changes to Written Rules

It's pointless even to attempt formal changes unless you derive them from a detailed understanding of the unwritten rules that are driving you.

Resulting Changes in Behavior

You are seeking harmony not just throughout your organization, but within your industry. That is the ultimate test of the unwritten rules.

Darling, it's me! I'm _so_ sorry, but I think I'm going to be late yet again tonight.

8
Breaking Free

Rebelling Against Conventional Wisdom

There's a conventional wisdom about how we are all supposed to address behavioral barriers to performance. It says that we must concentrate on changing shared values and beliefs, because anything else is just tinkering around the edges. It tells us that not only must we focus on changing values such as quality, by attacking them head on, but that we must not expect to see major change for around five years.

And the devout preachers of such wisdom tell us that we should be content to wait for such a long time, because modifying people's behavior is a slow process and we should consider ourselves lucky if we can alter it at all. Indeed, they profess that it is an arcane art and only those who have been inducted into the magic can really understand what is going on, let alone help us. Rather, I should say, *tell* us what to do, because we can no longer remain in control—however uncomfortable we become with the touchy-feely nature of their sorcery.

The orthodox wisdom tells us that if we want major and rapid changes in behavior, then the only way to achieve them is for people to feel that their jobs are on the line. So, we are supposed to engineer circumstances that will create a sense of urgency—let us be honest, a sense of fear—within the body of our organizations. And with that stick we can beat our employees into a new mindset.

The established dogma is a lie. Worse, it is a self serving and dangerous lie. It has become a myth that we have all been told for so long by so many people, that we in turn have passed it on to our own colleagues and so reinforced the apparent validity and common sense of the gospel.

But through our own experience we should all recognize that the creed is false. We all know of at least one example where there has been a rapid transformation of behavior within an organization because of a change in the reward policy, or the opportunity of a promotion, or the relocation to a different building, or the introduction of voicemail, or the allocation of an insensitive new boss. We all know that it is possible for changes in written rules or top management actions and behavior to have fast and major repercussions on a business. It's only that usually these repercussions are totally unintended, uncoordinated, conflicting, and damaging.

Yet they show us that it is possible, indeed common, for some transformations in organizational behavior to happen fast, albeit as side effects to what was intended. The trick is to achieve the same changes by design, reinforcing each other, in alignment with overall goals, and as catalysts to corporate transformation. That is what mastering the unwritten rules of the game is really all about.

Consider the various case studies in the previous two parts of this book. There's a theme running through each of them. The common denominator is to focus on changing enablers and triggers but not what is important to people—the motivators—head on. Instead, encourage new behavior as a means to an end. Namely as a means of satisfying the original motivators, or of satisfying previously unsatisfied motivators. In time, people come to value the new behavior in its own right, and so you consolidate the transformation by an eventual, genuine change in values.

Because they are performance measures it's relatively painless to change triggers. It's often also relatively quick for people to respond to the changes—typically less than six months. It's a bit slower and a little painful to change enablers (because there you are changing the power structure of your organization and inevitably that means that you take power away from some people).

But both of these—both of these—are far faster and far less traumatic than trying to change what is important to people directly. Than trying to change their values. In other words, than trying to change the motivators of the organization.

And yet think about that for one moment.

Traditional approaches to addressing these sorts of behavioral problems, or to changing corporate culture, all cling to the conventional orthodoxy. They *always* focus on changing shared values. They always try to change motivators. It's the only thing they can try to do, because there is no cause-and-effect built into the anthropological models. So they have to try to change the symptom *without changing the factors that make the symptom inevitable.* I would submit to you that that is why they have developed such a tarnished reputation.

They're trying to push water uphill.

Largely as a result, whole hosts of managers have become highly cynical over the last few years. So many senior executives that I talk with worry that they cannot really remove behavioral barriers. Or they worry that they have to relinquish control to some sort of touchy-feely magic.

But you know, once you understand what's going on, there's not really any magic any more. The vital insight is that *the problems caused by behavior are not soft*. They are not nebulous and intangible, and they are not understandable by experts in behavioral psychology. The problems are logical. And so are the solutions. So you're back in the driving seat.

But only if you rebel against the established purist doctrines. Of course we all want to aim for the perfect solution. Naturally none of us wants to compromise and go for something that's less than the best. Yes, the only deep seated, sustainable change is likely to be achieved when we manage to change people's genuine values regarding "quality" or "customer focus" or "business orientation" or "teamwork" or "company values." But we also need to inject a note of pragmatism.

We will achieve great improvements to performance if we get 100-percent implementation of a major initiative that is only 70-percent ideal. We will achieve nothing but frustration and growing cynicism if we get only 70-percent implementation of an academically perfect solution. Seventy-percent implementation means we do not make it. We fail. We do all the ground work but "the last 30 percent" never happens. We get nothing.

Instead, we must manage the tradeoffs between shooting for perfection and achieving something practical. After all, in essence, that is what true management is all about. Purist evangelists still insist that the rest of us are prostituting ourselves by concentrating on anything other than a protracted, tortuous, and expensive war of attrition aimed at changing what is important to people through a sanitized form of brainwashing. They find a certain lack of purity in the idea that the only particularly relevant measure of their work should be its impact to the bottom line. To all such gurus and their fervent disciples I have only one comment: "Will you please get real!" Achieving major change within the modern business environment is not an academic exercise. And organizations under pressure should not be treated as laboratory experiments. Purism out. Pragmatism in. Whatever *works* best, is what *is* best.

The Rules Are Dead—
Long Live the Rules!

"The Rules are a circle that never begins, and nobody knows where the circle ends."

Like a never ending cycle of reincarnation, the unwritten rules in a company never die. They only turn into something else. From the ashes of their destruction a new phoenix rises to take the place of the old. Nor would we want it any other way. Despite what certain managers with a peculiarly mechanistic outlook on life would prefer, every organization in the world is a creature of its unwritten rules. And remember, those unwritten rules are not good or bad, they are only aligned or misaligned with what the organization is trying to achieve. So we should never try to get rid of the unwritten rules in our organizations. Or try to force them to conform to the written rules. We merely need to realign them.

And realign them again. And realign them once again. It's never ending. The ongoing succession of change after change that the new wave of management thinking has encouraged in organizations will probably never leave us. I suspect that we are not, as some suggest, simply going through a period of rapid change that will subsequently settle down and be replaced by a period of consolidation—although this is what has happened in the past. Instead, I think that it may be more fundamental than that.

We are entering an era in which many companies are already trying to transform into organizations that can continue to rapidly evolve—"learning organizations" that will react to changes in the outside world or inadequacies they find internally, and mutate in order to compensate. They are seeking to turn an ability to change fast into a source of competitive advantage. And that will alter the rules of the business game forever. It means that no organization will be able to rest on its laurels any more with regard to change, any more than today it can with regard to any other key success factor in its business.

A manager will no longer be able to relax when she succeeds in implementing a major change, but will instead immediately have to seek the next challenge. Everyone's competitors will be aiming for the same goal of continuing improvement, so to slow down the pace of

140

change, the rate of responsiveness, will be self defeating. Some industries will adopt this pattern of continuous change quicker than others. But every industry is currently attempting it in one form or another.

As a result, everyone these days is getting excited about "change management." Experts are starting to formalize the sequence of applied techniques and methodologies that maximize the chances of achieving successful change. Those of us who spend all our time working in this field tend to enjoy the fact that we are addressing what feels like the fundamental frontier of future business—the "change management process" needed to implement a specific type of improvement initiative.

Yet, in reality, we are all working on the tip of an iceberg and the sun is rising. We are all busy concentrating on how to maintain the magnificent shining ice sculpture that we produced overnight. And, as the sun starts to beat down and melt our work, so we transform the sculpture into something even better, even sleeker. As we progress, we are refining our process for constantly adapting the iceberg into something beautiful. Learning how to constantly maintain its evolving beauty despite our inability to return the sculpture to its original form. We have not realized that the sea level is dropping dramatically. Beneath us is an order of magnitude greater task.

The change management process for an improvement initiative is in fact no more fundamental than an accounts receivable process or an inventory management process. It's vital, but it's not really basic, not truly fundamental, to the future of high performance businesses. Over the next decade we will have to address an order of magnitude more complex processes. We will have to learn how to manage a *portfolio* of major improvement initiatives all in parallel.

It is the difference between managing one research project, as opposed to a portfolio of research projects each of different complexity and risk, and all aligned with corporate strategy. The shift in mindset is comparable to the transition over the last 20 years in the automotive industry. There, the leading companies changed from developing one new automobile every seven years, to developing an overlapping stream of inherently flexible designs.

That is equivalent to what we are going to have to do with change. Already, sustained competitive advantage is no longer achieved simply by successful implementation of a given change initiative. With the accelerated cross-fertilization brought on by competitive benchmarking, an additional key differentiator has become the speed with which you can successfully implement change. Both success rate and speed are strongly tied to a third competitive factor: the magnitude of the change that you achieve. As we discussed before, magnitude of change has been one of the main drivers of Business Process Reengineering.

Change has become four dimensional. Many companies are already seeking competitive advantage by exploring three dimensions: success rate, speed of change, and magnitude of change. They are concentrating on how to improve the likelihood of implementation of their improvement proposals, how to accelerate change, and they are applying these techniques on major Business Processes Reengineering projects. The battle is set to add a fourth front of attack: parallelism.

The way to outflank your competition in the future will no longer be to focus on one type of improvement at a time. Instead, the real differentiator will be to pull off a variety of improvement initiatives all at the same time. Some will be local (maybe at the departmental level), some will be cross-business, some will be incremental change, some will be redesign, and a few may be rethink. Each will carry a different risk-reward profile. *That* is the fourth dimension of change.

Now, of course, conventional wisdom tells us to focus. Not to go for a scatter gun approach but rather a rifle shot. Aim to do one thing well rather than several things badly. But then, wouldn't we expect conventional wisdom to say that, if there had never before been a way to ensure alignment of multiple improvement initiatives? It does not mean that parallel change cannot be achieved. Only that it has proven overly complex in the past and has often lead to change fatigue.

But guiding alignment is exactly what mastery of the unwritten rules of the game is helpful for. And guiding a portfolio of change is precisely why it will become more and more critical. However clever and intuitive the most gifted managers are, few if any have ever demonstrated the ability to manage massive parallel change successfully. Too many things change at the same time. That is why mastery of the unwritten rules *has* to become a core management skill of the future. If you thought the last few years were bad, felt that it was hard enough to manage the rate of change and the scope of change that companies are currently attempting, or if you have seen enough failures to last a lifetime, then, in the immortal words: "You ain't seen nothing yet!"

Mastering the Unwritten Rules of the Game

To achieve mastery of the unwritten rules and as a result manage complex change, how and when do you apply the unwritten rules appraisal technique? The guidelines are the same as for someone trying to diet: little and often.

My colleagues at Arthur D. Little and I have successfully integrated the unwritten rules technique into a number of change processes. And there appears to be a common sequence to all of them.

First, focus on what's giving you an ulcer. Maybe your business performance is poor. Maybe you've conducted a client survey or an employee survey and don't like what you found. Maybe you've benchmarked your competition and you fall far short. Maybe you are receiving increasing levels of complaints, or maybe you are attempting a rapid, major change and you want to avoid problems—or you have already hit them. Whatever it is, decide what aspect of your business is currently your greatest cause for concern, and determine to do something about it.

Second, uncover what the unwritten rules are that relate to your business issue. In other words, conduct a standard unwritten rules of the game appraisal.

Third, use the appraisal to indicate what aspects of your business are out of alignment. It's this stage that guides you in tracking back to the root causes of the business problems in the form of misaligned strategy, process, resources, or organization. Now you know what kind of improvement initiative will be needed. These first three steps have all focused on *understanding* just what is going on, rather than doing anything about it directly.

The fourth step begins the process of *change* by deciding how to realign things. As we saw in the case studies earlier in this book, the complexity of this step ranges from the trivial to the massively intricate. It can be as simple as the CEO deciding to make an announcement, or as difficult as the decision to conduct a major processes rethink.

The fifth step is to decide how the decision made in step four will impinge further on the unwritten rules. If the actions proposed by step four are simple, then they will already have taken the unwritten rules into account. Indeed, they will have been selected in order to effect agreed changes to the unwritten rules. If, however, the proposed actions are highly complex—such as a process reengineering—then you are likely to need to conduct further detailed unwritten rules analyses. These analyses will focus on uncovering unwritten rules that could act as barriers to implementation of the new designs. You may then choose either to make tradeoffs in the design that reflect aspects of the unwritten rules, or else decide how to make changes to the unwritten rules themselves. In other words, you may choose to repeat steps four and five, but this time specifically to improve the chances of implementation of the changes decided the first time you went through step four.

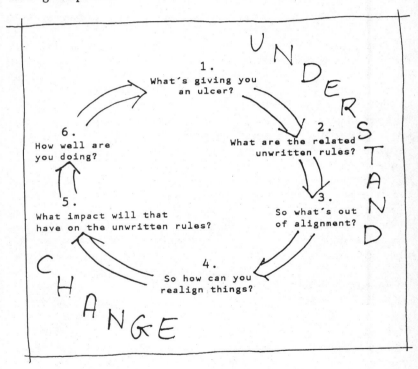

The sixth step is a check to see how well you are doing. Given the changes that you came up with in steps four and five, how well have they been implemented? Because it's easy to conduct a nondisruptive unwritten rules analysis, it's helpful to build a routine appraisal into the implementation phase of any change initiative. Wait for six months and then run an appraisal to see how much the unwritten rules have changed as a result of the change initiative. Have they changed as intended? Are there aspects of the change that are lagging behind and need a boost? Are there any unintended side effects that have occurred as a result of the change?

At the end of step six, you've come full circle. As a result of the routine appraisal, you may have come up with a new cause for concern, in which case you circle around one more time. Otherwise, you may feel that you have successfully addressed everything about the original business issue, and so you can address the next highest item on your list of ulcer-generating problems. And you circle around one more time.

You keep circling and you never end. That is the way that you can at last manage continuous improvement, not just continuous *incremental* improvement, but a portfolio of all forms of change. You keep circling around, each time picking off what feels like the most important issue that you want to address. At the end of each cycle you may choose a new issue, or you may remain on the same issue but change the function, or site, or level of the organization that you are focusing on.

That last statement becomes critical when you complete one cycle, and you realize that the greatest barrier remaining is top management itself, or maybe just the CEO. I don't pretend that the solution is easy, but at least draw comfort from the fact that the situation is a common one. Although, the best way to handle this problem is necessarily very dependent on the details, I'm frequently asked if there is any form of general guidance I can offer on how to handle the situation. So, let me suggest the generic approach that I've found works best.

Cycle round the six-step circle one more time, but this time addressing the business issue: "What are the barriers to implementation caused by top management or the CEO?" In other words, what you are doing is uncovering the unwritten rules and associated unintended side effects of the top managers themselves. You may sometimes choose to focus on a single individual, such as the CEO. Where the CEO is also a founder of the company, this is a common source of barriers.

The goal of the analysis is the same as any other. Namely, on the assumption that the managers are not incompetent, their blocking tactics must make sense—at least to them—even though they may not intellectually approve of them or possibly even be aware of them. Build up the usual links of cause and effect and then hold the mirror up to the managers.

Is this likely to prove politically sensitive? Yes, of course it is. However, I don't recommend the proposal made, only partly in jest, by one of my more insecure clients. Namely, that at this juncture you should conduct yet another analysis to understand the barriers to your feeding back the barriers to your implementing your original recommendations. Help ... This was all supposed to be driven by pragmatism. At one stage you need to fall back on political savvy and gut instinct for what will work. Only you can make the personal judgment as to where you should draw the line.

So what can you expect when you feedback to the top managers, or worse, to a single powerful individual? Well, I guess you could always get fired. No one ever claimed that this was a fair world. If you are honestly concerned about your security, bring in an outsider to conduct the appraisal. They're paid to be shot at.

If, however, you have no choice but to conduct and feed back the appraisal yourself, then draw comfort from this. I have been conducting unwritten rules appraisals for many years. I have frequently found myself in the role of hired mercenary, brought in to be shot at and sacrificed if necessary. I have never once suffered so much as a scratch. Admittedly, I have occasionally had to dodge quickly. But it's extraordinary the way things tend to work out.

One of my most memorable feedbacks was several years ago in a meeting to the head of one of the core businesses of a famous multinational. He had sat relatively quietly through the first quarter of an hour of my colleagues' presentation. Then he stood up: "Gentlemen, I don't believe any of this. You're mistaken." From what seemed a few inches away, he shouted: "It's all *horse manure!*" An interesting choice of phrase, but succinct.

The room was filled with all his direct reports, together with some of my colleagues, including my then boss, one of the grand old men of Arthur D. Little. All the managers from the multinational looked serious and murmured support for their boss. Mutterings began flitting around the room that sounded like the background chatter of a lynch mob. My colleagues too were looking serious, and if they had not been such consummate professionals they would probably have looked uncomfortable as well.

I decided that this was not the time for diplomatic niceties. "Don't risk making a fool of yourself, Winston," I said, registering a gratifyingly horrified reaction from everybody in the room. "There's only one person who's mistaken here: *You!*" I doubt that anyone had the presence of mind to drop a pin, but the room at that moment would have offered ideal conditions for listening to its descent. "You have such a forceful and charismatic personality that no one here is going to say a word against you." I waved my arms at his cohorts and spoke very quietly and compassionately. "The trouble is that, as a result, there's no one to stand up to you, look you in the eye and say, 'Winston, you're wrong.'" I stood up. "So it falls to me." I locked unblinking eye contact with him. "Winston," my voice started to rise, "I am here to tell you ..." my voice was becoming unusually harsh, "... that for once you are unadulteratedly ..." I built to a crescendo, "... unmitigatedly, utterly, and completely ..." I leant forward across the table and decided to end on a bellow, "... *wrong!*"

I could feel the blood vessels on the side of my neck bulging, so I held my pose for a few seconds so that everyone could appreciate the full theatrical effect. Winston broke eye contact and looked at his cohorts. They each avoided looking back at him. No one said a word. No one disagreed with what I had just said. He looked back at me. I smiled engagingly: "Now, can we get on with the rest of the presentation so that we'll all be in a position to decide what needs to be done?"

I sat down. The remainder of the presentation went without a hitch. An hour later Winston offered me a job. I almost ended up taking it ...

On other occasions, the feedback process could not be sweeter. There was a classic example a little over a year ago in the development division of an industrial corporation. This is by any measure a part of a business that requires controlled risk taking. Yet what we discovered was an unwritten rule in place that said: "Play safe, don't be seen to make a mistake." It was stultifying in its effect.

Where did it come from? From the misapplication of a frequently repeated phrase from the all-powerful CEO of the business: "Get it right first time!" When we reported this to the CEO he was flabbergasted. He responded, "When I went on about 'right first time,' I didn't mean it to apply to development." The next day he went and told everybody in the division what the confusion had been. Within days his organization was back in the development business.

His comment about the implied criticism of his management style? "This is the most powerful form of upward feedback I have ever had!" All credit to him. If you're a CEO receiving feedback, take note.

Flying the Flag

Four years ago, conducting my first appraisal in Taiwan, I realized how dramatically national culture can affect interpretations of unwritten rules. In the Far East, the desire to be part of a bigger group yet not lose face is all important. In Latin America, despite very hierarchical command-and-control structures, the unintended side effects can be very different from North America, because employees may genuinely equate themselves with the company. But even similar cultures create problems.

Consider Disney. They had great success in Anaheim and Orlando training employees to behave in ways that Americans consider wholesome. Their training worked in Disney Tokyo as well, but when they tried the same management techniques in Europe, they suffered from culture shock. For example, Disney has a ruling against facial hair (which always strikes me as a little odd considering that Walt Disney himself wore a moustache). Anyway, the written rule bothered some cast members. An unwritten rule in some European cultures says: "All written rules are *negotiable*." Similarly, the rule against the sale of alcohol struck the French as a national insult. In response, the president of the local authority pronounced: "The same Frenchman who'll go to Disney in Orlando and say it's 'fantastique' will describe Euro Disney as a 'cultural Chernobyl.'" The unwritten rule here was: "When in France, Mickey should drink as the French do."

In any event, trying to apply one set of written rules on people from many different national cultures produced some serious side effects—high employee turnover and low attendance at the theme park. Rules that worked so well in America and Japan initially failed to take hold in multicultural Europe. Even a company as sophisticated about culture as Disney did not accurately predict the side effects of their written rules. Many U.S. companies entering Europe hit the same sorts of barriers. The moral is, when cycling through the six steps proposed in the previous section, be sure to take national and local culture into account.

The Beat of a Different Drum

Television has given us two very different versions of a highly successful drama: the original "Star Trek" and the new show called "Star Trek, the Next Generation." In the United States you can watch an episode from each series every night on cable TV. If you put them side by side like that, you see a dramatic contrast in management styles of the two CEOs.

Captain James T. Kirk was a classic command-and-control CEO. In a crisis, if he wanted the U.S.S. Enterprise to fly faster, he would inevitably contact his chief engineer, Lt. Scott. "More power, Scottie! I need more power!" And Mr. Scott would equally inevitably give him immediate and urgent feedback: "I canna' do it, Cap'n. We're at warp Factor Nine as it is. She'll break up!" But Kirk would have none of it. He'd already snapped off his intercom.

Kirk did not see his role as worrying about feedback. Let alone to seek hidden side effects of his directives, caused by unwritten rules. His role was not even to think about feedback. His mission was to use the force of his personality to override any barriers, so that he could continue "to boldly go where no man has gone before."

But in the new series there is a new Enterprise, with a new captain—Jean Luc Picard—who has a new CEO style. One of the members of his senior management team is a counselor from a species known as Betazoid. Betazoids have a sixth sense that enables them to read some of the hidden motives and psychological currents running through a situation. In our terminology, they understand the unwritten rules.

And Captain Picard values the feedback. He does not override it. He seeks it out (even if it is hidden), absorbs it, and uses it to make an informed decision. That's a pretty good model for future managers. What's more, a manager preparing for the twenty-first century does not have to wait another 600 years to hire a Betazoid in order to understand the unwritten rules.

Riding the Crest of the New Wave

Several years ago I was having dinner with someone who is now the president of a massive multinational corporation. At that time, though, he was still having to prove himself by turning around one of the divisions. He's built like a bulldog and sometimes appears to have a personality to match. He was talking about accountability.

"I intend to make all my managers feel accountable, Peter. I want them to interpret my signals very clearly. When they do well they will be rewarded." His huge bulk leaned across the table as he planted his elbows on the table cloth, his face scarily serious. "And when they do badly ..." his voice dropped to a near whisper, "... they will be *punished.*"

Is this man a new wave manager? Absolutely he is. He was one of the first CEOs to appreciate the immense power of the unwritten rules to hold back an organization that is trying to change. There is nothing in the profile of the new wave manager that says that you cannot be tough, only that you need to be sensitive.

The two are not, of course, mutually exclusive. Only in the two-dimensional macho stereotypes portrayed by old-style Hollywood were they ever incompatible. The core skill of the new wave manager is to recognize that being tough is not the same as blindly forcing through a change even though it is in inherent conflict with the unwritten rules. That sort of management through brute force and ignorance just creates insidious side effects that these days have no time to work their way out of the system before the next wave of change creates even more problems. To manage in that way is like blindly thrusting your arm into an industrial food mincing machine and then pushing harder when you sense resistance. Very macho, but pretty stupid.

The most common reaction of those who make the transition is that they never look at things the same again or feel quite so isolated again. So, to help you to ride the crest of the new wave, here's a recap of the most important things I think we've learned over the last few years.

All You Need to Know About
The Unwritten Rules of the Game

What They Are

They're sensible ways to act, given the "written rules" and top management's behavior.

Written rules include all the formal aspects of strategy, process, resources, and organization. These, together with the actions and behavior of top managers, send signals into the body of a business. But factors beyond anyone's immediate control—national and local culture, economic climate, legislation, regulation, private agendas, existing unwritten rules—transform the signals into parallel unwritten rules.

They're neither good nor bad, only appropriate or inappropriate to what you want to achieve.

Each individual's day-to-day behavior is driven by a set of unwritten rules. Sometimes everyone within quite large groups all share the *same* unwritten rules, and everyone interprets a new policy statement or memo in the light of these shared unwritten rules. Yet it's senseless to pass judgment on the unwritten rules themselves. Whether they are appropriate depends solely on what you're trying to achieve.

Why They're Important

They often conflict with change initiatives, dramatically increasing your chances of failure.

There are three degrees of change—incremental, redesign, and rethink. As you move from incremental change at one extreme to rethink at the other, you increase the likelihood of introducing conflicts with unwritten rules. Management intuition no longer compensates—often because it's based on experience that no longer holds. Attempts to rethink without reflecting unwritten rules fail seven times out of ten.

If they conflict with changes that you try to force through regardless, you get severe side effects.

The harder you try to impose a change initiative in conflict with major unwritten rules, the further undercover the resultant negative side effects are forced to go. Of the nine common side effects, the most damaging are those that *are* hidden, causing people in the organization to appear to act in unprofessional ways. Yet, their behavior makes sense according to the unwritten rules. It's nobody's fault and you should blame no one.

If you don't deliberately resolve the conflicts, you force your organization into a death spiral.

Contemporary organizations have to implement wave upon wave of change initiatives. Unless you tackle the many conflicts with unwritten rules, you won't have time to remove the unintended barriers to performance before the next change creates more side effects. All these side effects will combine and reinforce themselves until the organization is saturated with conflicting unresolved side effects—"change overload."

How You Should Uncover Them

Use techniques that let you focus only on those rules that are linked to specific business issues.

In a five-day series of interviews, initially often with middle managers, you should discuss specific business issues then cluster the interviewees' views under three headings: *motivators* (what is important to people) are a detailed version of Maslow's hierarchy of needs; they drive the other unwritten rules clustered under *enablers* (who is important to people) and *triggers* (how people are measured or can get what's important to them).

Use techniques that indicate the links to specific misaligned written rules or top-management behaviors.

Motivators, enablers, and triggers derive from all the organization's written rules and management actions. Motivators relate to remuneration, job content, career progression, status, training, hiring, and firing. Enablers relate to job descriptions, organization charts, reporting lines, and sign-off responsibilities. Triggers relate to performance measures, milestone descriptions, evaluation charts, objectives, vision, and strategy.

What They Tell You

They explain failures caused by often apparently unconnected written rules or top-management behavior.

Uncovering the unwritten rules can provide a missing link in your understanding of what's going on. It allows you to reinterpret what you once thought of as "problems" as unintended negative side effects caused by inconsistencies between the written rules or top-management behavior and the changes you're trying to introduce. Without that insight you cannot foresee what the most insidious barriers to change are likely to be.

They explain how "excellence" actually works so you can effectively reproduce it elsewhere.

Uncovering the unwritten rules is more than just a way of putting things right. It's also a method of decoding success so that you can replicate it. Striving for major change, you need both to avoid creating new written rules or acting in ways that create unintended negative side effects, and to appreciate the *hidden* benefits of existing policies and procedures so you don't unthinkingly get rid of them.

They offer the only practical way of recognizing misalignment in the key drivers of a business.

If your strategy for meeting stakeholder needs is not in line with the processes in place to implement strategy, or your resources and organization are not all supporting the processes, misalignment creates unintended negative side effects. Only by using the unwritten rules to provide the missing link in your understanding can you locate the side effects and track back to what is causing them.

How You Make Them Work for You

They give a fresh insight into business problems, letting you remove barriers to what you want.

To highlight the unwritten rules component of a business problem, keep asking: "Unless everybody in the organization is incompetent, why did this problem ever occur in the first place?" Cycle through six steps. What's giving you an ulcer? What are the related unwritten rules? So, what's out of alignment? How can you realign things? What impact will that have on the unwritten rules? How well are you doing?

They help you make the pragmatic tradeoffs required to realign goals with reality.

You can modify triggers and enablers, but don't try to alter motivators; instead, find new ways to give people what is important to them. Changing performance measures (triggers) can be painless—people can respond in less than six months; it's slower and more painful changing the power structure (enablers). Both are far more practical than only trying to change what is important to people (motivators) head on.

Sparking
the Revolution

Understanding the unwritten rules of the game is no panacea. It will not solve all of your management problems. I would never suggest that you give up on the other approaches to performance improvement that you have adopted in the past and found valuable. I do not propose for a second that it is the only tool that you need for managing change—or even that it is the most important. Nor does it invalidate many of the more established approaches that others advocate. In fact, it is inherently complementary to most of them.

What is more, viewing your business from the perspective of the unwritten rules is no more right or wrong than viewing your business from the perspective of processes, or quality, or strategic business units, or stakeholder needs, or information. There are a large number of equally valid perspectives on business and each brings its own benefits and has its own shortcomings. The unwritten rules of the game perspective is no different: no better, no worse.

But … that said, for some reason there is something fundamentally new and exciting about the approach. It's not an extension of the normal ways that we have addressed business, so it provides us with a perspective that for the moment is fresh. It reflects on corporate culture but does not deal in generalities and descriptions, so it offers what for now comes across as pragmatism where previously we had to commit to a leap of faith. And it does get to the heart of something that is becoming very important to us all—change.

I don't fully understand why the approach is generating the reaction in managers that it is, but there is an extraordinary excitement growing among those who have learned to master the unwritten rules. Maybe it's because at last they really do feel that they're back in the driver's seat when it comes to managing change initiatives. As a corporate president recently put it to one of my colleagues at Arthur D. Little: "You know, at last I really feel that I'm back in charge."

Maybe the excitement is being generated because analysis that previously took people months now takes them weeks, and changes that once took them years now takes them months. A little while ago, a team was feeding back to its top executives the results of a one-week appraisal of the head office's unwritten rules. The team had just fed back their predictions of an unintended side effect that would damage managers' abilities to operate effectively. The head of Human Resources stood up and said: "Unknown to you, we've just completed an 18-month study that shows that we are suffering from exactly the effect that you've just explained. And we were wondering why it was occurring."

Maybe it's exciting because the approach has such general applicability or because people from all walks of life are starting to think about how to change the unwritten rules in their own environments. Everyone from high-ranking government officials to distinguished sports celebrities is finding that they too live by the unwritten rules. One of the top stars of the British football league periodically rings me up to discuss his latest problems in tackling the unwritten rules of the professional soccer game. At one of the leading business schools, a research fellow has chosen to dedicate himself to analyzing how unwritten rules impact the implementation of strategy, as part of a major four-year research program led by Dr. Lynda Gratton, an Assistant Professor at the London Business School. And when I visited Prague recently, I was told that organizations in the Eastern bloc countries *lived and breathed* by the unwritten rules.

Or maybe what's exciting people is just that the whole approach is such fun, so new, so different, so familiar, and so obvious, so straightforward that they do not need to see whether they believe in it. They really *did* know about it all along. They had just never worked through all the implications of what they already knew.

Whatever the reasons, there's growing excitement.

Yet what exhilarates me most is thinking of the implications as everyone starts to become sensitive to the unwritten rules. The implications not just on the acceleration or the sustainability of change, but the implications for change of management style itself, and the implications for what it will feel like to work in organizations that have realigned their unwritten rules so that the petty frustrations and hypocrisies have been removed. What will it feel like to work in communities in which local authorities and government departments have realigned their unwritten rules, so that when you have to deal with them you don't feel like you're being strangled by an endless supply of red tape?

The "greed-is-good-whatever-the-human-cost" philosophy of the 1980s is no longer acceptable—because at the end of the day it did not deliver the goods. I said at the beginning of this book that we would all end up having to view our organizations from the perspective of the individual, not necessarily because that philosophy was "caring" but because it was the only route to sustainable high performance.

Yet the real point is that everyone wants that change, wants to rebel against the past, wants to break the rules, wants a revolution. We all resent the unnecessary hypocrisies, frustrations, and unnecessary pain that we have all come to accept as inevitable within our organizations and communities. Every time that we make a positive strike to bring harmony to the unwritten rules, we strike a blow for freedom. Freedom from smoldering resentment because we cannot win in an unfair corporate environment where no one seems willing or able to improve things. Freedom from feeling torn apart because what we are told is good for our careers is not what our family really wants. Ultimately, freedom from an unnecessarily stressful and constraining environment that no one was responsible for creating. It just happened.

Deep down, everyone within every organization who has ever suffered from conflicts in the unwritten rules wants that revolution. When it comes, the revolution comes from within.

All it needs is a spark.

THE RULEBUSTER'S
GUIDE TO UNDERSTANDING
UNWRITTEN RULES

Don't Panic!

Guide to the Guide

The **RULEBUSTER'S Guide** explains in detail how you can uncover and codify the unwritten rules of the game within your own organization. It has proven the most resilient approach of many tried at Arthur D. Little. It is also a readily learnable technique.

I don't know why that sounds so pompous, but it does. Anyway, a quick recap of the key aspects of the approach: The appraisal is designed to bring to the surface the main unwritten rules that relate to specific business issues that are affecting your organization's business performance. In general, the kinds of issues that can best be addressed are those relating to process rather than content. Typically, they correspond to business questions that are prefixed by **how** or **why**, but not by **what**.

Just uncovering and codifying the unwritten rules would at best be of academic interest only. The appraisal does far more. The real power of the appraisal is that it uncovers the links between the unwritten rules and the business issues that are affecting your business performance. Even more importantly, the appraisal also uncovers the links between the unwritten rules and the written rules and management behaviors from which the unwritten rules of the game are derived. It's this overall chain of logical cause and effect—from initial business problems right back to management levers you can shift to effect change—that provides the guidance for you to remove barriers to change.

You can codify the unwritten rules and their links through a carefully constructed sequence of two-hour interviews. For a specific business issue, within a group all sharing broadly the same unwritten rules, you can if necessary conduct an appraisal within five working days. In the absence of any obvious reason to focus on a particular set of interviewees, the most productive source tends to be a horizontal slice of middle managers. Ideally, you should have two interviewers: one leading the interview, and the other in support.

So, what's in the guide? Part A covers the interviewing technique to employ during the appraisal. Yes, I know that you probably already pride yourself on your interviewing technique, but this approach may well be different to what you're used to. I trained the technique to a group of expert interviewers in Scotland last year. Despite being sent fax after fax before the training, warning me that the participants had a "very short fuse" and would "quickly be turned off by time wasted on interviewing skills," we happily spent the best part of two days practicing the technique. By the end they were getting very good at it. At the start, most of them were terrible.

Part B of the guide explores the sequence to follow in preparing for the appraisal and then in conducting the initial seven interviews. Part C explains how to conduct the mid-point team workshop, the next seven interviews, and the final team workshop at which you distil the unwritten rules and their linkages: to unintended side effects and to motivators, enablers, and triggers. Part D is an example of the output from an appraisal, which can then be used as the foundation for a top-management workshop to decide what actions to take to remove unnecessary barriers to performance.

By using this guide you can become a fully accredited Rulebuster. You can gain mastery over the unwritten rules of the game, and you can wield all the power that goes with that mastery.

But beware. There is a dark side to the power: As you gain greater and greater insight into the unwritten rules of your organization you may find yourself torn between two very different paths. On one path you use your newly won knowledge to remove the inherent conflicts and hypocrisies in your organization, and so improve business performance.

On the other path you use the knowledge for your own ends. You become manipulative and callous and you treat your colleagues like puppets that you can make dance to your own secret tune as you pull their strings with a hidden hand. Although overall business performance may suffer, your own performance according to your private score card dramatically improves. Can you feel the attraction?

Unfortunately, I've never really been able to take the dark side seriously enough to want to embrace it. Partly because raw power alone has never been one of my key motivators. When you get good at interpreting the unwritten rules, the true Machiavellis are so obvious that their actions seem a bit pathetic, and who wants to look like that? Yet, melodramatic as it sounds, it is a real risk. Indeed, anyone who seeks mastery of the unwritten rules runs a dual risk. Not only must you avoid succumbing to the dark side, but you must also avoid being assumed by others as being manipulative.

There is a powerful talisman against both these dangers: Be open. Be obvious and let everyone know what you want and why you are doing what you are doing. Leave no one in any doubt as to your motivation so that no one worries that you have ulterior motives. Make it clear when you are doing something as a means to an end. Never pretend that you don't use the unwritten rules. Instead, tell people exactly which unwritten rules you are using and why. In other words, be up front about everything you do.

To those who secretly like the idea of manipulation, but would rather not sink into the potential excesses and the loneliness of the dark side, follow the same approach as I just proposed. Comfort yourself with the thought that from one perspective you can think of that approach as the **ultimate** form of manipulation—because you are using the unwritten rules to achieve what you want, everyone knows what you are doing, and you are doing it with their blessing. How much more manipulative do you want to be?

Choosing the dark side potentially carries a high price. I know people who have fallen victim to the siren song of using their knowledge of the unwritten rules for the purposes of secret manipulation. At best they become powerful, but isolated and cynical. At worst they become lonely, embittered, lose their self-esteem, and get found out. It's a gamble that tends to be attractive to those motivated by power or by what it can get them. The clever ones always believe that they can fool everyone else so that no one realizes what they are doing. They rise to the intellectual challenge and believe that they will always be able to remain in control. They try the drug and get hooked. What they end up doing tends to be preeminently egotistical and selfish, but sometimes it makes them tremendously successful.

The choice is yours. Far be it from me to be sanctimonious. Anyone who truly masters the approach covered in this guide will be able to embrace the dark side with ease. Likewise, anyone who truly masters the approach will be able to find out those who are using the unwritten rules for their own selfish ends. There's a neat symmetry about all this that I like. I look forward to the most wonderful battles in the future between those who choose the dark side and those of us who fight for the right to be free of them. It promises to be a struggle between good and evil worthy of Hollywood. Give me anything but boredom ...

So, for good or for evil, for better or for worse, here is your gateway to another dimension:

PART A

Gateway to
Another Dimension

Shut Up and Listen!

The technique for conducting unwritten rules of the game interviews is different from most other types of interviews. The prerequisite is for the lead interviewer to develop empathy with the interviewee. Without this the interview tends to be hopelessly unproductive. The goal is to set the interviewee off on a stream of consciousness about the pressures he or she and others feel within the company and how these relate to specific aspects of business performance. The support interviewer is there to record the interview accurately by means of verbatim quotes, keep the lead interviewer honest during subsequent analysis, help facilitate the interview if the lead interviewer forgets something, provide the lead interviewer with feedback after the meeting, and often to observe the interview so as to learn the skill of being a lead interviewer.

Above all else, the most successful way of encouraging a stream of consciousness from the interviewee is for both interviewers to **keep very quiet**—a severe discipline for some of us. The support interviewer should generally always keep quiet and appear to play a passive role, with only an occasional comment thrown in, and most of those only in the form of encouraging support.

The lead interviewer should also keep quiet. Imagine yourself as an investigative journalist not as a manager or consultant: Offer little advice unless explicitly asked for it. The way to shine in these interviews is not primarily through displaying relevant knowledge (which usually is appropriate in other situations), but rather through understanding. Predicting what it must be like for the interviewee to cope with specific circumstances in the company carries tremendous weight.

Silence is also immensely powerful as a technique for pushing people over the brink into saying something that they would otherwise leave out. When they give a short reply to what you feel is an important question, say nothing in response. Look encouraging and wait. A silent, slow count to 10 seems to relieve the excruciating embarrassment of the silence. Promise yourself that you will speak once you reach 10. You rarely have to, because the interviewee tends to open up, often providing very helpful insights. As a rule of thumb: **Never speak within three seconds of the last sound made by the interviewee.** Even then, you may choose only to repeat the last phrase uttered by the interviewee, so as to encourage an elaboration of the comment.

I have found, having trained a wide variety of people to conduct unwritten rules interviews, that the three-second rule is the single most powerful technique that I have ever recommended. It turns loquacious dogmatists into attentive observers and pushy salesmen into empathic confidants. It's a principle that many top managers have subsequently sought to encourage throughout their workforce even when seeking information utterly unrelated to unwritten rules of the game. Keeping our ears and eyes open to what people actually mean is all too difficult in practice. We all tend to talk far too much and listen far too little. Those who know me would assure you at this stage that I speak from deep personal experience ...

Somehow, you need to strike a chord of common humanity with the interviewee. To encourage rapport, both the lead and support interviewers' whole attitude should be supportive and nonjudgmental. The fundamental premise for an unwritten rules of the game interview is that "Everything that you say and all the ways that you behave make sense, at least to you, and we understand. We would probably act the same way in your shoes." You may even reinforce that with, "Yes, I've experienced the same thing," or "We've had that problem."

If you disagree with an opinion, say nothing, but nod for the interviewee to continue. Occasionally though, you may violently disagree, or believe that the interviewee is saying things that you do not think even he or she believes. In that case, play devil's advocate and ask if some people would not disagree. Don't personalize or identify with the implied criticism or you'll destroy any empathy that has built up. The role of the interviewers at this stage is not to pass judgment but to understand why the interviewee thinks as he or she does.

While the interviewee talks, ideally over 90 percent of the time, the lead interviewer notes down what appear to be interesting points and tries in real time to work out the implications for behavior that follow from what the interviewee is saying. The interviewer should periodically paraphrase implied thoughts and feelings ("Did I understand you right ...?"), and rarely, but with caution, lead the interviewee by attempting to interpret deeply concealed core feelings. Get it right, and you leap forward; get it wrong, either because what you say is incorrect or because it's too much for the interviewee to admit to, and you must immediately employ soothing tactics. Apologize, if that's helpful, and turn the situation around by asking the interviewee to give you the correct interpretation of what he or she said. Next time you gamble that you have synthesized a core thought or feeling, preface your contribution by "I don't want to risk putting words into your mouth, but ..."

Where you need detailed clarification or you need to test a comment against what you have heard elsewhere, the lead interviewer should note the issue, usually on a separate sheet of paper, rather than divert the flow of the conversation. Already on this sheet should be all the issues raised by previous interviews or from debriefing external consultants. Throughout the interview, the lead interviewer should take any opportunities that arise to effortlessly steer the conversation to focus on these issues without disrupting the flow of the interviewee's monologue.

Usually, you can steer the conversation by word association. For example, the interviewer may be talking about teams and use the words "team structure." The lead interviewer has departmental organization as an issue to be discussed, so he or she might say: "OK, we've been talking about team organization, but what about how the departments themselves are organized?" Handled in the right way and at the right time, the blatant change of subject seems like a free association of ideas and the interviewee often doesn't recognize what has happened. Indeed, a common (albeit indirect) feedback from unwritten rules of the game interviewees is: "It was fun, but all I did was talk; there was no structure whatsoever. I'm not sure that we'll get anything concrete from the exercise."

Occasionally you may need to nudge the conversation in a new direction and resort to doing so in an obvious way. Doing that more than a couple of times is a mistake because it will tend to constrain the interviewee too much. Real-time analysis of implications for behavior, together with undetectable structuring of the interview, are the most difficult skills of conducting an unwritten rules of the game interview. So, training should concentrate on practicing these skills.

Of course, it would be lovely if every interviewee were warm, friendly, and helpful. But let's be honest. Some are a real pain. Interviewing these happy souls is what stops unwritten rules appraisals from ever becoming boring. For, as every unwritten rules troubleshooter knows: When the going gets tough, the tough get ... empathic.

Nervous, Irritated, or Machiavellian?

The interviewee may be sweetness and light. Alternatively, the interviewee may turn out to be the devil incarnate. So, you always start the interview the same way. Confirm the context for the meeting and the timing and reassure the interviewee that all comments will be unattributed in any feedback. It may sometimes be helpful to add that "Only a few key individuals in the company have been selected for interviews." Be careful though that the interviewee does not then worry that there is some ulterior motive for being selected ...

The interviewee should have had a short memo to set the scene and request the interview, so usually this part of the meeting can be relatively short. However, don't rush it, because it's an ideal time to evaluate the interviewee's style, expectations, and concerns. On the basis of your first impressions of the interviewee, you must quickly select, and then convey back, the impression of yourself that you believe is most likely to build rapid rapport. What's more, it's only in these first few minutes that you can talk very much, so you have only a short time to get across the image you choose.

Occasionally, the interviewee will launch straight into a monologue prefaced by the words: "I've had a few thoughts about what the unwritten rules of the game are around here." This is great because it usually signifies that the interviewee is one of the 10 to 20 percent of people who seem to be able to verbalize the unwritten rules unaided. That can be a tremendous short cut. Just sit back and listen. Nod and murmur encouragement, but don't interrupt the flow.

The most common response after the initial introduction, however, is for the interviewee to say: "Fine, I'm all yours. Fire away." An easy way to respond is to focus on the specific aspect of business performance that the appraisal is designed to address. Simply say: "What we're really trying to do is get a feel for what it's like to work in X, particularly with respect to [aspects of business performance]. You know: how the system actually works, what you consider to be important, that sort of thing. Maybe we could start off just talking around that, and then we can zero in on areas of interest as they occur."

Usually that's enough to set the interviewee talking. If not, add something like: "OK, for a middle manager in X, who are the most important people with respect to [aspects of business performance]?" "What drives them?" "What are their most important measures?" If those gambits fail, stop trying to force the interviewee to generalize. "Forget about anybody else, specifically for you, what is most important to you, what drives you?" "Who is the most important person in the company to you, particularly with regard to [aspects of business performance]?" "What are the most important things that happen to you?"

If all these approaches fail, fall back on a more direct approach: "Let's leave that for the moment. Just tell me your own thoughts about [aspects of business performance]." The main disadvantage of this approach is that the interviewee tends to churn out a well-worn monologue on the subject that inevitably suffers from having originally been designed for public consumption within the organization. Forcing him or her to address the subject from a different angle tends to provide a far fresher, and so revealing, portrayal of the issues.

Sometimes, about 20 to 30 percent of the time, interviewees don't seem to want to tell you anything useful. They may talk a lot, but it sounds like the "official story" or else the words they think you want to hear. They don't say anything very controversial: nothing very good, nothing very bad. Unfortunately, many of the classic interview techniques for resolving this situation, such as interrupting and pointedly restating the question, are inappropriate, at least for the first half of an unwritten rules of the game interview. They risk damaging rapport. Instead, try to empathize with why the interviewee is acting that way.

In such situations, the interviewee tends to be one of three types: cautious or nervous, bored or irritated, or Machiavellian. The nervous interviewees have what they believe is a valid reason not to open up about something. Ultimately, they don't trust one or both of the interviewers to keep what they hear confidential. The irritated interviewees don't think the interview is worthwhile. The Machiavellian interviewees think that they gain competitive advantage by understanding the unwritten rules of the game and are damned if they are going to share that with anybody.

The initial approach with each type is the same: namely, for the lead interviewer to try extra hard to build a rapport. To aid this process the support interviewer needs to fade into the background and become completely silent and unexpressive. It may help to stare mainly at notes rather than the interviewee. The intention is to encourage empathy, using eye contact and body language, between the lead interviewer and interviewee. It's important for both interviewers to look calm, relaxed, and confident.

For the moment, the support interviewer should continue to take notes. Only if the interviewee wants to say something "off the record" should the support interviewer immediately, without any fuss, lay down the pen and quietly look up. When the interviewee is in two minds whether to continue, the last move tends to increase the pressure to continue, because everyone is expectant and it's apparently off the record. After an appropriate delay, while the interviewee's eyes are on the lead interviewer, the support interviewer can quietly resume note taking.

If rapport builds, the nervous interviewee may slowly start to thaw out and divulge sometimes highly sensitive information. The first time this happens the response should be one of high interest and support. Similarly, the irritated interviewee may feel able to hint at his or her skepticism about the process, allowing the lead interviewer the opportunity to take time out of the interview to explore and with luck diminish the interviewee's concerns.

Machiavellian interviewees only rarely respond to rapport building. Indeed, they can become snide, flippant, or even obnoxious. Under these circumstances do not rise to the bait, otherwise you'll lose any opportunity to benefit from the interview. Let it all wash over you. Be clinical about observing what is going on. Smile. Consciously relax your jaw; it's painfully obvious when someone is smiling and gritting their teeth at the same time. Remind yourself how wonderful it is that you're being paid at the same time as being insulted. Think whatever thoughts are necessary to prevent the interviewer from getting under your skin. Don't think that even though you are seething you will be able to hide it from the interviewee; it's exceptionally difficult to mask the body language of anger and the interviewee will pick it up, if only subliminally. Your only defense is genuinely not to take the situation seriously. Frequently, this approach results in a grudging respect from the interviewee, and ironically you manage to build rapport after all. Sometimes you can then goad the interviewee into boasting about the clever ways that he or she, usually portrayed as "other people," behaves in certain situations. Achieve that ... and you've beaten them at their own game.

All Good Things Come to an End

The value of what the interviewee tells you often increases as rapport builds, with the best toward the end of the interview. Sometimes you find that in the last half hour an interviewee will really open up. She may revisit a topic originally discussed over an hour before, but this time it's fleshed out, given a different slant, elaborated. Sometimes interviewees will genuinely see things differently by the end of the meeting, and will want to qualify something that they said earlier.

So pace the interview to avoid a wild rush toward the end to work through outstanding issues. Rushing comes over as heavy handed and destroys the opportunity for a fluid conversation that throws up some nuggets of information at the end of the interview. Better to leave issues outstanding.

Above all, be sensitive to any issues that the interviewee may be toying with sharing. Sometimes there is a major topic of concern that the interviewee is reticent about. Sometimes there's a critical insight lurking just under the surface of the interview like a subtext to the whole conversation. If you're hamfisted or indifferent because you're tired after conducting four interviews in one day, then you'll miss your opportunity. On the other hand, if you remain consistently responsive and sympathetic, you have the greatest chance of peeling away yet another layer of facade just before the meeting ends.

Naturally, though, never run over the allotted time. Two hours tends to be far longer than most other interviews, and to take even more can be seen as insulting. If, unasked, the interviewee offers to continue, that is a different matter. Leave time at the end of the interview for "any other points," and then leave the door open for the interviewee to get in touch if he or she suddenly thinks of something highly relevant in the bath.

That covers the basics of how to get people to open up. Now, how do you conduct the appraisal?

PART B
Voyage into the Unknown

Preparing to Open Pandora's Box

The unwritten rules appraisal around a specific business issue comprises a minimum of 14 interviews and two interview-team workshops, followed by preparation of documentation, feedback, and a top-management workshop to decide what actions should be taken to remove barriers to performance. Under pressure, you can do the actual appraisal part in five days, provided you expect that the group you are interviewing all broadly share the same unwritten rules. If you're trying to distinguish two or more sets of unwritten rules, for example in two divisions of the company, you will need more interviews—about 10 more for each extra set of rules. You can conduct a 24 interview appraisal in a week, but it will need either two well-coordinated interviewing teams or else very long working days. I once had to do 28 two-hour interviews in four working days—most of them without a support interviewer. I can't say that I recommend it.

The 14 interview appraisal splits into three parts:

- Preparation
- Appraisal
  First seven interviews
  Mid-point team workshop
  Second seven interviews
  Final team workshop
- Documentation, feedback, and top-management workshop

It's primarily the structure of the interview program and the dynamics of the interviews themselves that makes it relatively easy for you to distil the unwritten rules and their linkages both to problems and to management levers for change.

If you need to slot the interviews and team workshops into one week, you can schedule them as follows:

First Seven Interviews

Monday

9:00 -10:00   *Optional*   Public presentation on
                                            the unwritten rules of
                                            the game

11:00-12:00   Interview #1   Phase I: Confirming the
                                            key question

1:00- 3:00   Interview #2 ⎫
                           ⎬   Phase II: Surfacing
3:30- 5:30   Interview #3 ⎭   related issues

Tuesday

8:30-10:30   Interview #4 ⎫
10:30-12:30   Interview #5 ⎬
                           ⎬   Phase III: Fleshing out
                           ⎬   the issues
1:30- 3:30   Interview #6 ⎬
3:30- 5:30   Interview #7 ⎭

Mid-Point Team Workshop

Wednesday *(early to mid-morning)*

7:30-11:00   Workshop #1   Phase IV: Selecting
                                            important behaviors

Second Seven Interviews

Wednesday (late morning and afternoon)

11:00- 1:00 Interview #8	Phase V: Understanding
2:00- 4:00 Interview #9	cause and effect
4:00- 6:00 Interview #10	

Thursday

8:30-10:30 Interview #11	
10:30-12:30 Interview #12	Phase VI: Confirming
	understanding
1:30- 3:30 Interview #13	
3:30- 5:30 Interview #14	

Final Team Workshop

Friday

8:30-12:30 Workshop #2	Phase VII: Codifying the
	unwritten rules
3:00- 4:00 *Optional*	Initial feedback session
	to top management

Alternatively, if your travel schedule permits, you can start the appraisal on Thursday, hold the mid-point workshop over the weekend, and then finish the appraisal during the following week. This takes the pressure off, and may be an attractive option the first few times you run an appraisal.

In the following few sections, we will work through each phase of the appraisal in turn. But before we do, let's look at what you need to do prior to kicking off the interviews. A few weeks before the appraisal, ask the local top management to select interviewees who are representative of the environment you want to study. If in doubt, suggest a focus on the middle management as the most productive hunting ground and frequently the group suffering most from side effects of the rules. If external consultants are already familiar with the organization because they have previously worked on site, it can be very helpful to debrief them before you start the appraisal. You can sometimes construct a candidate set of unwritten rules and side effects from their anecdotes. This saves starting from a blank sheet of paper.

Before you start the interview program, obtain thumbnail sketches of the interviewees, and guidelines for handling them—pet peeves, key concerns, and so on. The local top management should send out memos to the selected interviewees, explaining what the interview program is about and requesting a meeting. Also, the memo can invite them to attend a presentation on the unwritten rules of the game to be held before the set of interviews starts. Ideally, the memo should explain the basic concept of the unwritten rules of the game. The description may stimulate potential interviewees to think, before their interview, about what they see as the unwritten rules. Sometimes, however, it's inappropriate even to mention unwritten rules, because people in the organization perceive behavioral problems as "too soft an issue to be taken seriously." You can then position the interview as aimed at understanding barriers to implementation of an improvement initiative or barriers to business performance.

When scheduling an appraisal, remember that conducting one over a month is more difficult than completing it in one week because it is far more difficult to pick up patterns in what the interviewees tell you. For the same reason, when using parallel interviewing teams, it is far better for each team to concentrate on interviewing a group that they believe will share broadly similar unwritten rules (for example, on the same site or in the same function), than to spread their time across two or more populations.

So, enough preparation. Let's get going.

Pain Is the First Step to Enlightenment

Kick off early on Monday morning, perhaps by presenting a one-hour overview of the unwritten rules of the game to members of the organization, including those about to be interviewed. The introduction will save time during the interview, and stimulate interviewees to think about what they can contribute. You are now ready to conduct Phase I of the appraisal: confirming the key question (interview 1).

Ideally, your first interview should be with a senior local sponsor. The aim is to confirm the business context in which the work is to be conducted. Understand which problems are giving top management pain—what is agravating the sponsor's ulcer? Remember, unwritten rules are not good or bad—they're just appropriate or inappropriate given what the organization is trying to achieve. So, to conduct a pragmatic appraisal, you need to position it within a business context.

Keep this initial interview to about an hour. It's the only interview of the appraisal that does not use the unwritten rules of the game interviewing technique. Approach the interview just as you would a conventional business discussion. You're not trying to uncover unwritten rules, although you may pick up some pointers. Instead, you are trying to understand the business risks, and the barriers to business performance, that are of concern to line managers and that might be caused or exacerbated by conflicts between written and unwritten rules. In other words, you are refining your understanding of why it is worthwhile looking at the unwritten rules of the game in the first place.

Sometimes you'll be asked to address fundamental problems such as difficulties with the product development process. Other times you may be offered what are passed off as root causes of the fundamental problems such as poor teamwork, no cross-functional cooperation, short-termism, no creative risk taking. They're not truly root causes, of course, but at least they suggest the linkage from unintended side effects to overall business problems. Sometimes only the root causes are mentioned, and they are never explicitly related to overall business performance at all. However, whether they are stated or not, the impacts of such side effects on business performance are usually obvious to all concerned and can often be taken as read.

The prime deliverable from the first interview, therefore, is an understanding of how to position the project so that line managers see it as relevant and pragmatic. But you also need to understand the context sufficiently so that you can use your **business judgment** during subsequent interviews to distinguish what is important and what is noise. This is one of the main things that stops an unwritten rules of the game interview from degrading into a general evaluation of the social norms of the organization. Each interview is primarily **issue driven.**

People sometimes ask me: "But doesn't that mean that you will come up with a different set of unwritten rules depending on the business issue you happen to select?"

Yes. That's the main reason for focusing on the business issue in the first place. It allows you to come up only with detailed unwritten rules that are relevant to what you are trying to change. Otherwise you would be swamped. There can be hundreds of unwritten rules within an organization. You do **not** want to codify them all. You really don't. Fortunately, however, experience shows that you always seem to come up with the same major unwritten rules whatever business issue you are addressing. So, when you subsequently create changes to some of the unwritten rules, you are pretty well guaranteed that they will still prove compatible with the bulk of the rules that you are leaving alone.

However, focusing on a business issue implies that during subsequent interviews you will be employing a great deal of implicit knowledge that you have about your industry. Whenever you make a judgment about what is noise and what is important, you will draw on a wealth of experience about how a business functions. So you need to have that knowledge to start with. People with little knowledge of business do not make good unwritten rules of the game interviewers.

What's more, knowledge tends to be industry specific. Be careful: In the past, some practitioners of the unwritten rules of the game appraisal felt that because they had become highly skilled in applying the technique within their own company, they were clearly capable of applying it in another company, or even another industry. They found they weren't as hot as they thought.

For the rest of the appraisal you will always relate what people tell you back to this first interview. It all starts with pain. Now you set out to find what's causing it.

Lost at Sea

You are ready to begin Phase II of the appraisal: surfacing related issues (interviews 2 and 3). This will be your first unwritten rules interview; prepare to feel a little lost—it's normal. If you have had the benefit of debriefing your colleagues or external consultants on any unwritten rules they have noticed in the organization, and any potentially negative or positive side effects they may have on performance, you will have some idea of the issues surrounding the key question agreed in interview 1. Otherwise, you start with a blank sheet of paper.

Use the standard beginning for an unwritten rules of the game interview: introduction, positioning (based on interview 1), and rapport building. Do what you can to get the interviewee **talking** for two hours. Do not expect any great insights to leap out at you during the two Phase II interviews. You may be lucky enough to hit upon an interviewee who can paint a vivid picture of what it's like to work in the company, what some of the key unwritten rules are and where they cause problems. More likely you will not. Simply note down all the related issues that the interviewees talk about.

You will end up with a laundry list of motivators, enablers, triggers, unwritten rules, problems possibly related to unwritten rules, and lots and lots of stories that may or may not be relevant. It doesn't matter. At this stage you are getting a feel for the company, and collecting stories and examples to which you can refer obliquely in subsequent interviews to encourage interviewees to open up.

However confusing the outcome of the day's interviews, don't let it worry you that you're lost at sea. Remind yourself that it could be worse—you could be drowning.

But long before you find yourself drowning in a sea of apparently unrelated data, you **will** start to see patterns. Trust me.

Starting to See Something

It's Tuesday morning. Overnight your subconscious will have started to filter out the noise from what you heard on Monday, leaving you ready to start Phase III of the appraisal: fleshing out the issues (interviews 4, 5, 6, and 7). Even if you conducted the Phase III interviews with no further preparation, you would probably automatically find yourself looking for evidence around a set of issues that arose the day before.

However, to make sure, spend a few minutes before the first interview to list, from memory, the four or five main issues that arose the day before. Check them against your notes. You'll find that you can construct the list far faster on Tuesday morning than on Monday night. If you have parallel interview teams, construct the list together—over breakfast can work well.

Start the interviews as usual, maybe by kicking the discussion off around one of the issues on your list. Appear nondirective, but steer each interview over all the issues. Avoid discussing solutions; focus on problems. With only a small number of issues you should cover them all comfortably in two hours, so you can choose your moment to nudge the conversation. You are unlikely to have to redirect the interview in an obvious way. Add to your list of issues as new ones arise.

Having all the Phase III interviews on the same day has the advantage that the comments of the four interviewees blend into each other. You will find that your brain starts picking up patterns in what the interviewees tell you. As you reach interviews 6 or 7, you may be starting to see consensus among your interviewees on various issues. You may even be recognizing some of the nine common side effects discussed earlier in the book. Or you may not. If no pattern is emerging, then (as it clearly states on the title sheet of the Rulebuster's Guide) **Don't Panic!** The mid-point team workshop is designed to give you and the rest of your team an opportunity to stop interviewing and start talking about just what it is people have been saying to you.

PART C
Writing the Wrongs

Filling Up
Flip Charts

Think about the structure of the appraisal like this: To help codify the unwritten rules and their side effects, the objective of the interviews in the second half of the appraisal (Phases V to VII) is to test hypotheses suggested by the interviews in the first half (Phases I to III).

Sometimes in Phases I to III you reach a point after one of the interviews when everything seems to gel and you can see some of the motivators, enablers, and triggers, their unwritten rules, and the resultant side effects. Sometimes you hear about symptoms that correspond so well to one of the common side effects highlighted earlier in this book that you are immediately able to set up a hypothesis of what is going on. This usually happens when you have been talking to one of those uncommon individuals who can verbalize the unwritten rules unaided.

At other times, the transition is gradual, with rules and side effects hinted at in the Phase II interviews coming into focus from then on. However, if none of these transitions has occurred naturally by the half-way point, don't worry. It will happen automatically as a result of Phase IV of the appraisal: selecting important behaviors (the mid-point team work-shop). At this session the interview team forces itself through the discipline of pulling together an unstructured candidate set of unwritten rules and perceived problems.

Start early on the Wednesday morning, or spend time on Tuesday evening, with all the interview team present to discuss what they have learned. The team needs all the interview notes and two flip charts; you have three and a half hours. A pot of strong, black coffee can help.

The support interviewers play back from their notes what they consider to be the pertinent issues they heard. The lead interviewers chip in with relevant extra detail or comments on process, for example, why they nudged the interview along and what they interpreted from the response, or what additional implications they now draw from the interview. To make sure that the workshop does not become a talking shop, whoever is facilitating the meeting should insist on disciplined feedback, with discussion only on points that appear relevant. This filter on the feedback makes it easier to prioritize issues. As each issue is raised, the facilitator should write it down on a flip chart under one of two headings: "rules" or "problems."

Under the rules headings, note all the unwritten rules that interviewees have mentioned: all the pressures to act in a given way that are beyond the interviewees' power to change. Typical unwritten rules might be: "Keep your boss happy," "Keep job hopping," "Don't be associated with failure," or "Make sure the right people see you." Despite pressure, of course, individuals may choose not to conform. What is significant is that the pressure exists.

At this stage, do not worry about chaining unwritten rules together, or about distinguishing unwritten rules from the motivators, enablers, and triggers that are driving them. For instance, "Keep job hopping" may be the sensible unwritten rule people derive from a motivator, such as career progression. What's more, there may be another rule, "Keep your eyes open for a good job," that is itself derived from the rule to "Keep job hopping." But in this workshop you need not build these chains of cause and effect. Instead, just record three rules: "Keep job hopping," "Do what's needed to progress your career," and "Keep your eyes open for a good job."

Seriously damaging behaviors that act as major barriers to improvement are rarely the direct result of unwritten rules. Instead they are usually side effects, often caused by conflicts between unwritten rules and written rules. For example, chronic short-termism is seldom the result of the existence of an unwritten rule that says "Only think very short term." It is usually the result of a clash between an unwritten rule, "Keep job hopping," and a written rule, "You're only rewarded for the current performance of your department." Likewise, most organizations are unlikely to have "Undermine teamwork, but do it secretly" as an unwritten rule. If, however, the written rule says "Teamwork is important to the organization," while the unwritten rules say "Stand out as an individual if you want to progress," then people may be so busy standing out as individuals that teamwork cannot happen.

Indeed, it's uncommon for unwritten rules to be directly damaging to performance. Most people will not tolerate working under such conditions for long and the conflict is usually quickly resolved. As a rule of thumb, you will find that when interviewees talk about problems, or disconnects, or barriers to performance, they are more likely to be highlighting side effects than unwritten rules. These probable side effects are what you place under the heading of problems.

Be careful: Don't assume that a behavior you have previously come across in a different organization as a side effect is perceived in the

same way by your current interviewees. For instance, in some estab-
lishments, people may "Play safe and avoid taking chances" because a
written rule, "People don't move from department to department,"
reinforces an unwritten rule, "Maintain your standing with your peers."
Employees may feel no direct pressure to play safe, and indeed might
strongly resent the idea, but they behave that way anyway.

In a bureaucratic government organization, however, playing safe
may well be an unwritten rule in its own right. Here, employees feel a
definite pressure not to take risks and quote "Play safe" as an
unwritten rule. Although they may not consider the unwritten rule itself
to be negative, they may observe negative side effects such as lack of
innovation or unimaginative solutions as being direct consequences of
the otherwise neutral unwritten rule. In some financial institutions,
"Play safe" may be a written rule enshrined in a formal policy document.

Although it is often appropriate to focus on perceived negative side
effects, you may be using the appraisal to decode success, rather than
understand problems. Then, you need to highlight unintended positive
as well as negative side effects. Similarly, even in an analysis aimed at
decoding failure, you may also come across many positive side effects
that need to be maintained or amplified. For example, the unwritten
rule "Be seen as a contributor to the group," might have the positive
side effect of "Recognition acts as a powerful nonfinancial motivator."

A major oil and gas company recently found just this when they
conducted a rules of the game analysis on one of their oil fields. They were
convinced that the hard nosed drillers and maintenance operators only
responded to money. But the analysis very quickly showed that the field
of 170 people was actually like a small village: Everyone very much cared
about what their peers thought of them. So peer recognition was a key
motivator. As a result, any public pat on the back carried a disproportion-
ately high prestige. Until the analysis was conducted, managers had
treated the employees as a tough crowd who would neither welcome nor
respond to such nonfinancial rewards. When the managers tried out a
more balanced approach, they quickly discovered that they had been
missing a major opportunity.

Trying to maintain the distinction between rules and problems, work
through the notes for each of the seven interviews. Every time a rule or
problem is corroborated from another interview, put a tick next to it on
the flip chart. The more ticks for a given issue, the greater the corroboration. If separate issues are obviously associated, note the linkage on the
chart but do not get hung up on structuring; that's the task of the final
team workshop.

R U L E S

Do what can to progress career✱
✓✓

Keep boss happy ✓✓✓✓✓

Protect your own turf ✓✓✓

Keep job hopping✱✓✓✓✓✓

~~You should hop till you're 90~~
You're out at 45 ✓✓✓✓✓
Don't leave the U S A   ✓✓✓

Make sure you stand out of crowd
✓✓✓✓

Keep your quarterlies high
✓✓✓

Don't be associated with failure
✓✓✓✓✓
Make sure you survive job cuts ✓✓
Get some Friends at Court ✓✓✓✓
Keep eyes open for good job
✓✓✓✓

P R O B L E M S

Chronic short-termism ✓✓✓✓ #2
  (long term is 2nd Quarter!!)
~~Backstabbing~~ (no corroboration)
No one takes any risks* #3
                      ✓✓✓

V. long lead times**
  (It takes forever)   ✓✓✓✓✓

Products are boring*
           ✓✓

Departments		
Functions	}	Don't work **
Divisions		together #1

    ↓
         ✓✓✓✓✓
worse

Teams don't work properly ✓✓✓
                         #4
only the best or worst people
are willing to go abroad
  ✓✓

Aim to get through the interview notes in about two and a half hours. On the flip charts, you should now have listed several rules and problems, all with one or more ticks beside them to show that they have been corroborated in other interviews. If you don't have two healthy lists, then postpone the afternoon interviews and call in some experienced help—something has gone seriously wrong. Hopefully, though, your flipcharts will look something like the two shown on the following pages. In practice, you are likely to have covered several sheets. Ten to twenty rules and slightly fewer problems is typical.

A couple of weeks after writing these words I got a plaintive phone call from one of my colleagues in Caracas. He was running his first mid-point workshop and was worried that the whole process was taking too long. His team had begun working though all the interview notes, trying to characterize each of the quotes as either a rule or a problem. But the exercise was proving laborious and mind numbing. What could he do? What should you do if you find yourself in the same bind?

Relax. Stop being so mechanical about the process. Try putting all the interview transcripts to one side and continuing from memory. Try writing down on the flip charts what your instinct tells you are the most important unwritten rules. Use your business judgment to select from memory the most damaging problems that you came across. And only then go back to the interview notes and work through them to see whether there is corroboration for what you have put on the flip charts. This can be a tremendous short cut. It's a lot easier to test a hypothesis developed by your subconscious than it is to derive the hypothesis mechanically from raw data. Take advantage of the heavy data processing that your brain has already conducted.

Assuming that you are satisfied with the two lists, spend the last hour of the workshop preparing for the second seven interviews by agreeing what hypotheses you need to test. First, if you have not done so already, decide how many populations you are dealing with. In other words, how many distinct groups in the organization have noticeably different unwritten rules of the game. For example, high flyers versus the rest, or division A versus division B. You'll be able to do this partly by considering the flavor of the unwritten rules: Where the rules appear different for different people you may have a new population. Also, think about any "them and us" situations you may have, for example between the parent company and a recent acquisition.

In general, see if you can reflect differences in unwritten rules or side effects simply by including qualifiers in the wording. For example, "Don't spend too long away from HQ, unless you're a high flyer," or

"Keep job hopping, unless you are in R&D." If you can get away with such simple qualifiers, then initially hypothesize that you are broadly dealing with only one population. If, during later interviews, you find that high flyers consistently operate to a different set of unwritten rules from everyone else, then you will have to prepare two sets of unwritten rules in the final team workshop. If you find that, even at this stage, you cannot reconcile the unwritten rules of two or more populations, then reevaluate the number of interviews needed for the appraisal.

Once you have agreed how many groups of people you are concerned with, prioritize the list of problems in order of perceived risk or opportunity to business performance. Exclude any problems that have not been corroborated. Spend the last few minutes brainstorming links between the highest priority problems and the unwritten rules on the other flip chart. It's those links that you will try to understand better during the next phase of interviews.

During the first half of the appraisal, you confirmed the context in which the appraisal was to be conducted, and uncovered a set of business issues relating to it. By the end of the mid-point team workshop you will have hypothesized how many different sets of unwritten rules there are in the organization, what the main unwritten rules relating to the business issues are, and what their effects are on performance.

During the second half of the appraisal, you will clarify the motivators, enablers, and triggers, see how they are interpreted in terms of unwritten rules, and understand how the rules lead to unintended positive and negative side effects. By the end of the final team workshop, you will have agreed on a first-order approximation of the unwritten rules in the organization that are relevant to the problem being addressed, and you will have developed the chain of logic that shows how the problems affecting business performance are being created.

You are now ready to proceed with the second seven interviews of the appraisal. At this stage, with the mid-point workshop successfully completed, you will probably feel that you and your team have all earned a really stiff drink. Unfortunately, it's still only 11 a.m. I never said it was that easy.

Making
Good Connections

Now you can begin Phase V of the appraisal: understanding cause and effect (interviews 8, 9, and 10). From here on your aim is to deepen your understanding of the unwritten rules and how their associated side effects may affect performance. In particular, what you want to do is understand why the side effects are natural consequences of the unwritten rules. This requires a slight shift in emphasis from the preceding interviews.

As you start each interview, use some of the (unattributed) examples and stories you heard during the first half of the appraisal to encourage interviewees to burrow quickly into detail. These interviews seem to have a strange dynamic: Now that interviewees realize that other unnamed individuals have told you some of the more sensitive unwritten rules and side effects, they feel far more willing to elaborate. You can start talking about sensitive issues within a few minutes rather than the hour it took in earlier interviews, although some interviewees may still be unable or unwilling to tell you much that is helpful.

During the interviews, you can now begin clustering rules under statements about motivators, enablers, and triggers. A motivator statement ("What is important to me") tends to cover the rewards and penalties embodied in such things as remuneration, status, job content, and career progression. Examples are: "The greatest reward is to be seen as a leading authority in your field," or "... to earn as much money as possible," or "The greatest penalty is to be sidelined," or "... to be fired."

The motivators are the carrots and sticks to which the interviewee responds. They may not, however, be the same as the carrots and sticks that the company is using to try to improve performance. For instance, a research establishment trying to motivate employees by remuneration, when job content is what turns them on, is missing an opportunity just like the managers of the oil field referred to in the last section. Motivators are written as statements of fact because they're "givens" that the interviewee has no power or desire to change. There tend to be many unwritten rules that are directly driven by the motivators. They reflect the natural ways to behave implied by the motivators themselves.

The motivators, together with the unwritten rules implied by them, drive all the other unwritten rules. For every distinct attribute listed in the motivator statement, there is likely to be an enabler, usually a person but sometimes technology, that can grant that aspect of reward or impose that type of penalty. The enabler statement ("Who is important to me") tells you who the enablers are in a particular case. Examples are: "Your line manager dictates your annual salary increase," or "Only a senior vice president can sponsor your job transfer," or "Any of the department heads can veto a budget," or "Your peers can lobby for or against you," or "Access to the computer network is the only way to know what's going on."

For every motivator-enabler combination, there is likely to be a trigger, for example a performance measure, that brings the appropriate enabler into force who then grants the motivator. The enabler statement ("How I am measured," or alternatively "How I go about getting what is important to me") tells you what the various triggers are for a particular group of interviewees. Examples are: "You are granted a promotion—or sidelined—based upon the current profit or loss of your department," or "... according to the success of your team," or "... according to how well you are doing the things that should lead to success in a few years time," or "... according to the quarterly share price of the company," or "... according to the perceptions that the various senior vice presidents have of you," or "... according to how well you delivered on what you promised."

Often a company's formal, official, written rules match some aspects of the motivator, enabler, or trigger statements. For example: "We aim to provide our employees with stimulating, long-term careers in sanitary inspection" (motivator), "Your line manager dictates your performance evaluation" (enabler), "The formula for calculating the performance related pay scheme is ..." (trigger).

Other aspects of motivators, enablers, and triggers may be derived from top managers' behavior or other sources that are in no way written down. For example: "The organization always looks after it's own" (motivator), "Being a member of the country club is important if you want to get ahead" (enabler), "Provided you reach your quota you can get away with murder" (trigger).

Some aspects may come from factors largely beyond anyone's control, such as national and local culture, external regulation and legislation, economic climate and people's private agendas. For example: "It is important to be respected by your local community" (motivator), "Whichever political party is in office specifies the top three levels of the organization" (enabler), "People can't leave while the job market is so poor" (trigger).

During interviews 8, 9, and 10, encourage your interviewees to spend time talking explicitly about motivators, enablers, and triggers as they perceive them. What you are trying to do is to get a new perspective on the perceived problems in the organization. You need to start viewing them from the perspective of the unwritten rules. That way, you can reinterpret the problems as unintended negative side effects caused by conflicting rules.

By the time you get to the end of this long day, comprising the mid-point team workshop and the three Phase V interviews, you will have learned enough that tomorrow you can start playing it all back to your remaining four interviewees.

But for now, sit back, relax, and pour yourself that long, stiff drink.

Leading
the Witness

Thursday. You have eight hours of interviews left. This is Phase VI of the appraisal: confirming understanding (interviews 11, 12, 13, and 14). In these final interviews, your aim is to pin down why, if at all, unwritten rules are producing side effects that act as barriers to performance. To do this, you need also to understand how the unwritten rules lead from motivators, enablers, and triggers.

Kick off the meetings by playing back some of the motivators, enablers, triggers, and side effects that you have unearthed, and asking for confirmation. During the interview, draw the interviewee out on how particular motivators, enablers, or triggers are linked to the unwritten rules, and how these in turn cause some of the perceived side effects. Inevitably you are leading the witness, but by the Phase VI interviews your goal is no longer to try to uncover new unwritten rules, but rather to better understand the rules you have already uncovered. The interviewer technique is, therefore, more participative than before.

You are looking for a clear hierarchy of cause and effect. The motivators, enablers, and triggers imply sets of unwritten rules. For instance, "Keep your boss happy" might derive from the enabler statement "Your boss dictates all your key rewards and penalties." "Keep your boss happy" is, therefore, an enabler rule.

"Keep job hopping" is a motivator rule, derived from the motivator: "The greatest reward is to get broad experience in the company as quickly as possible." This combination often occurs in companies that have had a written rule "You can only get the top jobs if you have breadth rather than depth of experience within the company."

It's important to take care in categorizing unwritten rules. You need to ensure that you correctly link them to motivators, enablers, or triggers. What's more, you must register whether the unwritten rule follows from all aspects of a given motivator, enabler, or trigger, or only selected parts. So, in the example, the motivator rule "Keep job hopping" is only driven by the part of the motivator statement that advocates broad experience. It would in no way be linked to another part of the motivator statement such as: "It's very rewarding to have the respect of your colleagues."

Other implications of the motivator "The greatest reward is to get broad experience" could include "Don't get too specialized" and "Avoid staying too long in the same job or you will damage your career." The latter sounds like a trigger rule—related to the trigger for a penalty— rather than a motivator rule. However, **because it is driven by a motivator, you should categorize it as a motivator rule.** That is purely pragmatic, because it makes your life a whole lot easier later. If at this stage of the appraisal you have not gotten one of the motivator, enabler, or trigger statements quite right, you may subsequently have to refine it and all its associated unwritten rules. So the aim is to categorize by cause-and-effect, rather than by some kind of academic taxonomy.

In practice, few unwritten rules are derived exclusively from a single motivator, enabler, or trigger. For instance, the unwritten rule "Don't worry about the long-term implications of your (in)action because your past will not catch up with you" is an understandable inference from the trigger statement "You're rewarded or penalized only according to the current performance of your own department" and the motivator rule "Keep job hopping."

So, try to see the inferences from the interviewee's point of view and think through the logical links between motivators, enablers, triggers, and behavior. Try to understand whether, for example, the trigger statement is driving the behavior more strongly than the motivator statement. Are people thinking short-term because they will be moving on soon or because they are rewarded only for the here and now? If your interviewees seem to feel that constant job hopping is the real driver, then you should classify the unwritten rule as a motivator rule. Either way, annotate the unwritten rule to show its strong links to both motivator and trigger.

During each interview, it may be helpful to clarify your thinking by sketching out specific linkages you are finding, as seen in the diagram on the facing page. These links will provide you with the keys that you need to finally unlock the secrets of Pandora's box.

```
MOTIVATORS        Unwritten rules
  Broad
experience        Keep job hopping (1)
(via promotion)   Not too specialized
                  Avoid stay too long(2)
etc.
etc.


ENABLERS                  Avoid failure
Line boss                 Keep boss happy
(for promotion)           Stand out
Peers
(for respect)     ~~Don't be pushy etc.~~
                  Be member of old boys
etc.              club


TRIGGERS
Your P&L                  Protect own turf
(for boss)                Watch quarterlies
                                        (3)
? for peers       Don't be pushy etc.

SO: [NO ONE] ~~does it~~ thinks strategically!
                  (comes from 1,2 and 3)
```

Pulling the Rabbit
from the Hat

Friday morning, and at last you are ready for Phase VII of the appraisal: codifying the unwritten rules (the final team workshop). This is when you appear to pull a rabbit out of an empty hat. Psychologically this is a good move, because your local client support interviewers may by now be beginning to worry that you have just been holding open-ended discussions all week. Then suddenly you appear to conjure up something specific in front of their very eyes. During the workshop you distil, with them, the unwritten rules of the game for their business, together with side effects acting as barriers or catalysts to performance.

Of course, in reality, you've been building up to it all week by following a highly organized program designed to structure the unwritten rules and their associated side effects. So, by the time you get to the final team workshop you have done almost all the hard work. The workshop is an opportunity to document and to build ownership of what you have already confirmed in the Phase VI interviews.

As in the mid-point workshop, gather the whole interview team. You will probably need at least four hours. If you are worried about time, make a good start on the workshop the night before. The model you should use during the workshop to structure your findings is as follows:

- Motivators, enablers, and triggers correspond to, but are rarely the same as, the written rules; a set of motivator statements drive the enabler and the trigger statements.

- Each of the sets of motivators, enablers, and triggers has associated unwritten rules; when an unwritten rule is derived from more than one motivator, enabler, or trigger, it's classified under the motivator, enabler, or trigger that most strongly drives it.

- There may be side effects caused by conflicts between rules; these are categorized with the motivators, enablers, or triggers that drive them most strongly.

Start by creating three flip charts entitled respectively: motivators, enablers, and triggers. Stick them high up on the wall of the room you're using. If the walls are covered with expensive wallpaper, this may prove an embarrassment later. Create three more flip charts, each with the heading: unwritten rules. Place one under each of the sheets already on the walls. Finally, produce three more sheets, this time called: side effects. Place these beneath the six sheets that are already up. I did tell you to put the original sheets **high** up on the wall ...

You should now have a three-by-three matrix of sheets. If there's not room on the wall, or if you find that by now you cannot reach the top sheets, you will have to take them all down and rearrange things. I don't know what deep psychological need this process satisfies, but some of the best interview teams I have worked with have happily spent the best part of half an hour arranging and rearranging sheets until everyone present was satisfied. I guess it has something to do with team building.

Anyway, when all the bonding is over, start listing the motivators, enablers, triggers, unwritten rules, and side effects that you have heard over the last four days. Check interview notes as you go, to ensure that everything that people said is represented, as well as corroborated by others. The more contentious an issue, the more corroboration you need. The ultimate test is: "Is putting it in the list justifiable in light of what we **actually heard** in the interviews?"

At this stage of the workshop, ensure that only well substantiated comments get through to the next round. In the document of record, you will eventually need to include unattributed verbatim quotes from interviewees. These will act as evidence for the unwritten rules and side effects that you judge are important, omitting comments not substantiated by others. The number of quotes on a given topic usually reflects the number of occasions that the topic arose throughout the interviews. This does not, however, directly indicate the support for, or perceived importance of, a statement. Often a subject on which there is consensus is rarely mentioned, because it's "taken as read."

However good the workshop facilitator, as you start listing everything people will start talking about what could be done to improve things. Do not lose these burning solutions. Write them on yet another flip chart for **later** discussion when you consider the next steps.

When you have agreed on what has been heard in the interviews, start to structure what is on the flip charts. Begin with the motivator, enabler, and trigger statements on the three top flip charts. Tidy up what you have written, if necessary replacing the sheets. Do the same with the unwritten rules beneath them. Stand back and consider the motivator, enabler, and trigger statements again. If you had never spoken to anyone in the company, but had simply been presented with the three sets of statements, would you see the links? Is every part of the motivator statement echoed by corresponding parts of the enabler and trigger statements? Are there any other logical implications from the motivators, enablers, or triggers that you have not included? When you consider any two sets in combination (i.e., motivators combined with enablers, combined with triggers, and so on), are there further unwritten rules that appear logical but are missing? If so, did any interviewees refer to them, albeit in an oblique way? If no one said anything, would it be useful to dig deeper later, as part of a more detailed appraisal?

Now tidy the lists of negative or positive side effects to each column of motivators, enablers, and triggers. As with unwritten rules, categorize side effects according to the motivator, enabler, or trigger that interviewees saw as the main cause of the problem. So you might categorize "Chronic short-termism," "No interest in strategy," and "No concern that errors from the past will catch up with you" as motivator side effects: driven more by motivator rules (i.e., "Ensure each promotion is to a different part of the organization" and "Avoid damaging your career by staying in one place too long" than by trigger statements (i.e., "You are only rewarded for the current performance of your department"). It's not always so complicated. In another organization, the same chronic short-termism might simply be driven by one trigger, "You are rewarded according to the quarterly share price of the company."

Categorize side effects caused by inconsistency between written rules and unwritten rules according to the unwritten rule. So, you might classify "Secretly undermine teamwork" as a side effect of the enabler rules, because it is the result of the inherent conflict between the formal trigger statement, "Teamwork is important to the company" (an implied trigger for reward), and the unwritten enabler rule "Stand out as an individual if you want to progress," which derives from the enabler statement "The senior vice presidents alone select outstanding individuals for transfer." In practice, the written rule "Teamwork is important" might have a corresponding unwritten rule such as "Be seen to espouse the teamwork ideal" (a trigger rule). In that case, as for unwritten rules, you would annotate the side effect to show it was derived from two sources.

When you've tidied up the categories, then—surprise, surprise—you've finished. If you have time, you can begin attaching quotes to support the analysis. Or, you can prepare for an optional preliminary feedback session that afternoon with your local sponsor, probably the person from interview 1. For that you can just neatly rewrite the flip charts you have. For everyone else you will need something better.

Climbing into the Driver's Seat

Whatever oral feedback you provide at the end of the appraisal, the main feedback is a written report based on the final team workshop. It is the basis for a top management workshop to decide what action to take as a result of the appraisal. The report provides you and the other managers with the means to climb into the driver's seat of change. An example of a typical report is shown in the final part of this guide.

Before you work through that example, let me explain a bit about the format. An appraisal report usually has a short introduction, followed by an executive overview of the motivators, enablers, triggers, implied unwritten rules, and perceived potentially positive/negative side effects, followed by several pages of supporting quotes, structured under the headings used in the executive overview. If the focus of the appraisal has been to understand **barriers**, then you may choose not to list any positive side effects. But that always seems a bit of a shame.

You'll see from the example that there is a referencing system throughout the report. Although it can seem a bit daunting to start with, it's actually very simple and it can save a tremendous amount of confusion during the top-management workshop. Here's how it works: Everything related to motivators, enablers, and triggers is prefixed by an M, an E, or a T respectively, so you can immediately tell the derivation of an unwritten rule or side effect. A report usually references many motivators. The one that interviewees **feel drives their day-to-day behavior** the most is M1. The next is M2, and so on. It's often not possible to rank the motivators with great certainty, but you should aim to maintain an overall trend toward weaker motivators. You should never have more than nine motivators. Three to five is typical.

The enablers and triggers are numbered **so that they correspond to the motivator that is driving them**. In other words, E1 is the enabler that can grant the motivator M1. T1 is the trigger that will cause E1 to grant M1. For example, if M3 is "Respect (from your peers)," then E3 could be "Peers (for respect)" and T3 might be "Perceived profile (by peers)." Rigor with this numbering makes it far easier to check logical coherence of the motivator-enabler-trigger relationships.

Unwritten rules are numbered so that their primary derivation from a particular motivator, enabler, or trigger is obvious. So, T31 is the first unwritten rule associated with the trigger T3. T32 is the second unwritten rule associated with the same trigger. For example, if T3 is "Perceived profile (by peers)," then T31 might be "Don't be seen to be egocentric" and T32 might be "Always appear helpful to your colleagues." If possible, the unwritten rules that interviewees feel are most powerful are numbered first; typically you do not have more than three unwritten rules associated with a given motivator, enabler, or trigger. If you find unwritten rules that are not clearly derived, then prefix them with MO ["em-zero"], EO, or TO depending on whether they relate generally to motivators, enablers, or triggers. So, TO2 would be the second non-specific unwritten trigger rule.

Potentially positive side effects derived from motivators, enablers, or triggers are prefixed M+, E+, and T+, respectively. Potentially negative side effects are prefixed M–, E–, or T–. Positive and negative side effects are numbered with the most important side effects first. M–2 is the second most damaging negative side effect derived from a motivator. E+1 is the most beneficial positive side effect from an enabler. After each side effect, the unwritten rules from which the side effect is derived are listed with the most important drivers first. In the following sample report, for example, M–5—"Poor relationships with clients"—is annotated M22, M32, M52, M41, T11, M21, M11, E53, TO2, T53, T51, T52 indicating that it's driven most strongly by the motivator rule M22—"Avoid staying in a particular job too long"—and least strongly by various trigger rules, including T52—"Keep your quarterlies up." Of course, the relative strength of the derivations is very subjective, but the trend should be toward weaker drivers toward the end. You may choose to cite around 10 unwritten rules for a single unintended side effect.

When adding quotable quotes in the latter part of the report, you may find that far fewer support a given unwritten rule or side effect than you thought during the final team workshop. If so, check all your notes to see whether they remind you of interviewees' comments that you did not write down. Be careful. Resist the temptation to start becoming creative and adding quotes that interviewees **should** have said. Either note on the report that further work may be needed to corroborate the issue, or dismiss it. Finally, read the quotes under each unwritten rule and side effect. All the quotes rarely support exactly the same message, so cluster them to lead the reader through a sequence of thoughts that elaborate the overall heading. Then, check that all the quotes support the heading. You may want to suggest to the rest of the interview team a refinement to some of the wording of a particular unwritten rule or side effect.

That's the theory.

So, what does it all look like in practice?

PART D

Analysis of
an Alien World

A Report for
Ghee Formulates
Unwritten Rules of the Game
Pilot Appraisal

The Ghee Legacy

Background to
Ghee Formulates

In order to place the unwritten rules of Ghee Formulates into an historical context, it's helpful to consider just how the company was founded. Its early years are typical of many other companies that have likewise become household names.

In 1919, Robert McGregor Ghee, of Scottish-Indian descent, landed in New York as an immigrant. He brought with him a secret formula that had been handed down to the eldest son of the chieftains of the clan McGregor ever since the early sixteenth century. Robert was actually only a nephew of the current chieftain, and this was one of the main reasons he left his homeland so soon after learning the formula from his eldest cousin during a three-week drinking marathon.

The formula itself was for the secret additive to turn ordinary malt whiskey into a highly efficacious medicine, guaranteed to cure a wide variety of ailments including distemper and ringworm. At a poor neighborhood in Manhattan, Robert set up a small factory in the corner of his rented bedroom. To start with, sales of his Ghee Whiz Elixir were not very encouraging. But, after a year of near poverty, his business demonstrated a miraculous upturn.

From 1920 to 1933, Robert became a billionaire. Interestingly, his company's golden age corresponded almost exactly with the years of Prohibition in the United States. By the end of the 1920s, his newly incorporated Ghee Formulates was producing a whole range of alcohol-based products, from the still massively popular Elixir to a unique type of rocket fuel that had not yet found a market. However, in 1935 Robert decided to diversify. As he was a keen amateur radio ham, and by now owned several glass bottle factories, he decided that an obvious area for expansion was thermionic valves. This led to entry into the growing electronics market, and the eventual divestment of all the alcohol-based businesses. The rest, of course, is history.

Tell Me About It

Introduction

This document contains the findings of an unwritten rules of the game pilot appraisal for the contract R&D businesses of Ghee Formulates in New York. Ghee Formulates R&D undertakes cutting edge electronics and computing projects for US and international clients. Its major laboratory facilities and corporate headquarters are in New York. Smaller laboratories, originally developed on the back of large client-specific projects are based in Edinburgh, Munich, and Taipei.

The pilot appraisal was based on one week of interviews conducted by members of the GF High Performance Task Force from xth-xth Xxxxxxxx, 199x. The task force was asked to focus on unnecessary barriers to high performance. All but one of the 14 interviews were of two hours duration. Each of the interviews had a member of the task force present. Interviewees were drawn as far as possible to represent each contract R&D division, primarily at the intermediate level.

The executive overview comprises the set of motivators, enablers, and triggers and derived unwritten rules highlighted by the task force in a closed workshop held on xth Xxxxxxx, and based exclusively on the evidence gathered during the preceding week. The overview also includes unintended side effects for high performance **as perceived by interviewees**. On the basis of the small sample of interviews, there was insufficient evidence to indicate substantial differences between the unwritten rules for the three divisions, although nuances and differences in emphasis are likely to exist.

The remainder of the document comprises a selection of verbatim quotes from interviewees, structured by the motivators, enablers, triggers, unwritten rules, and side effects to which they relate. Each of these has only been included in the analysis if it was well supported by quotes from several interviewees. As a result, many apparently interesting comments have been omitted because they were not substantiated by others. In general, the number of quotes on a given topic reflects the number of occasions that the topic arose throughout the interviews. This does not, however, directly indicate the level of support for, or perceived importance of, a given statement. Often, when there is a very high level of consensus on a subject it is rarely spoken about because it is taken as read. More quantitative ranking is not possible in such a short appraisal.

A Quick Look

Executive Overview: Motivators

Period: Current **Grade:** Intermediate **Category:** NYHQ

N.B. Unwritten rules can, in principle, **all** be beneficial, although side effects and conflicts may create barriers to high performance.

Motivators

M1 Keeping your job until you're 45 (given recent spate of downsizing)

M2 Getting to the top of GF (which needs broad experience across R&D)

M3 Respect (from your peers within GF)

M4 Exciting work (intellectually exciting)

M5 Money (through high individual bonus)

Associated Unwritten Rules

M11 Conform to profile of business oriented ambitious achiever

M12 Almost no one survives past 50

M13 In your early 40s start planning an exit route if you're marketable

M21 Ensure each promotion is to another part of R&D

M22 Avoid staying in a particular job too long

M24 Constantly keep your eyes open for your next job in R&D

M31 Make sure your colleagues know your achievements

M32 Don't worry too much about external profile

M41 Avoid doing the same type of work twice

M42 Be available at the right place at the right time

M51 Do the things that will increase your personal bonus

M52 Don't worry too much about things that don't get measured

Consequent Potentially Positive Side Effects for High Performance

M+1 Collegiate environment with constant cross-fertilization
     (M31, M11, M22, T41, M21, M24, E41, T22, E21, E31, E32)

M+2 Well rounded employees with clear focus on specified goals
     (M21, M22, M51, M52, M42, M32, T41, T53, T52, E31)

Consequent Potentially Negative Side Effects for High Performance

M–1 Nobody tends to think strategically
     (M21, M22, T52, T53, M11, M12, M13, M51, M52)

M–2 Chronic short-termism
     (M51, M24, M22, M21, M52, T52, T53)

M–3 No one is concerned about long-term consequences of their (in)action
     (M52, M51, M21, M22, T52, T51)

M–4 Self-fulfilling prophesy that employees over 50 are unproductive
     (M12, M13, T41)

M–5 Poor relationships with clients
     (M22, M32, M52, M41, T11, M21, M11, E53, TO2, T53, T51, T52)

Executive Overview:
Enablers

Period: Current   **Grade:** Intermediate   **Category:** NYHQ

N.B. Unwritten rules can, in principle, **all** be beneficial, although side effects and conflicts may create barriers to high performance.

Enablers

E1   The Ghee family and functional chiefs (for firing)
E2   The Ghee family (for rapid promotion)
E3   Peers (for respect)
E4   Functional chiefs (for exciting work)
E5   Your line boss and your boss's boss (for individual bonus)

Associated Unwritten Rules

E01   Never let anyone see you fail
E11   Never get on the wrong side of the family
E12   Never displease the functional chiefs
E21   Do everything to join the "in crowd"
E22   Nothing is more important than pleasing the family
E31   Earn your "club membership" by proving your loyalty
E32   Socialize with colleagues out of work time
E41   Keep in constant touch with your function
E51   Keep your line boss and your boss's boss happy
E53   Stand out from the crowd, but not too much

Consequent Potentially Positive Side Effects for High Performance

E+1   Mutually supportive environment
      (E31, E22, E32, E21, E11, E12, E51, M42, T21, T32)
E+2   Possible to get occasional major job through extremely fast "as favor"
      (E22, M11, E11, T23, E12, E51, E01, M42, E53, T32, M51)

Consequent Potentially Negative Side Effects for High Performance

E–1   Long lead times—caused by poor cross-company cooperation
      (E53, E51, T51, E01, E12, M52, T15, E11, M51, M22)

E–2 Clients find solutions solidly professional but unexciting
(EO1, E12, E11, TO2, M32, M52, M41)

E–3 Inability to leverage senior skills
(E53, M41, E51, TO2, T51, E12, T41, M51, M32)

E–4 Voice mail overload saturating everybody
(E53, T22, TO2, E41, M31, E31, E11, E12, T41, M11, TO1, T13, M24)

Executive Overview:
Triggers

Period: Current   **Grade:** Intermediate   **Category:** NYHQ

N.B. Unwritten rules can, in principle, **all** be beneficial, although side effects and conflicts may create barriers to high performance.

Triggers

T1   Correct profile (to avoid being fired)

T2   Perceived value to firm (for family)

T3   Perceived profile (by peers)

T4   Technical competence (for functional chiefs)

T5   Current financial performance of your current group (for line boss)

Associated Unwritten Rules

TO1   Build credit with all key influencers and power brokers

TO2   Play safe

T11   Avoid leaving the United States

T12   Declare ambition

T13   Espouse team orientation

T14   Never sponsor anything alcoholic to the family

T15   Never appear too loyal to line managers in front of functional chiefs

T21   Be associated with the family's pet projects

T22   Give high-profile presentations and feedback

T23   Do the family unsolicited favors

T31   Don't be seen to be egocentric

T32   Always appear helpful to your colleagues

T41   Be seen as an expert

T51   Protect your own turf

T52   Keep your quarterlies up

T53   Get contracts for your own group now

Consequent Potentially Positive Side Effects for High Performance

None mentioned.

Consequent Potentially Negative Side Effects for High Performance

T–1 Teamwork does not happen
(T22, T51, T41, T53, E53, M51, M52, all despite T13 and T31)

T–2 Only the best, the worst, or the over 40s are willing to go abroad
(T11, TO2, TO1, M42, T22, E41, T41, M24, M31, T23, M12, M13, E32)

T–3 Inadequate diversity
(TO2, T12, T41, M11, T32, T31, T12, T13, M12, E11, E12, E32)

T–4 Standards, rigor, and corporate memory have all gone down
(T53, T52, T51, M41, M52, M22, EO1, E22, M12, all despite TO2)

Qualifying Quotable Quotes

Rules and Side Effects with Supporting Quotes: Motivators

Period: Current   **Grade:** Intermediate   **Category:** NYHQ

N.B. Unwritten rules can, in principle, **all** be beneficial, although side effects and conflicts may create barriers to high performance.

Motivators

M1 Keeping your job until you're 45 (given recent spate of downsizing)

"We all like working here."

"No one wants to leave if they don't have to."

"There's something special about GF."

"Like the rest, I'll stay on until my mid-40s."

"Why go before you have to?"

"Most of us love it here."

"Suddenly you can't take your job for granted any more."

"Time was when you automatically assumed a career at Ghee."

"Times have changed."

M2 Getting to the top of GF (which needs broad experience across R&D)

"We're all very ambitious."

"I want to get to the top like everyone else."

"We're all supposed to be ambitious, and in general we are."

"The ultimate accolade is to make it to the top."

"Coffee with the family every Sunday morning—I could get used to that!"

"I look at the life top management lives and I think: 'That's for me.'"

"Stretched limo, corner office, part of the inner circle."

"I guess if I'm really honest, I'm hungry for the top."

M3   Respect (from your peers within GF)

"Respect is extremely important—respect from your peers and superiors within GF."

"One public mention from a member of the family and you're golden."

"There is no greater reward than being mentioned in the State of the Union Address."

"We want to be seen to be successful in project work."

"People want their colleagues to think of them as dependable."

"Everyone likes to win a star project award."

"The award ceremony is really rather something."

"It feels good to be seen as successful in casework."

"Perceived success in casework is a reward in itself."

"We all seek respect."

"I really want my fellows to think I'm worth something."

"Our colleagues are the best judges of our worth."

"If your peers don't respect you, then who will?"

M4   Exciting work (intellectually exciting)

"We're all here for the intellectual stimulation."

"Give me something interesting to do and I'm happy."

"People here want the electronic equivalent of a crossword puzzle."

"We like solving challenging problems."

"It's like being in academia but you're well paid."

"If the work ever got boring I'd be gone."

"All I want to do is be creative."

"Give me an intellectual challenge!"

M5   Money (through high individual bonus)

"You can get a healthy individual bonus. Pushing that up is a real motivator."

"Provided that I don't sacrifice the fun of the job, then I want to make as much money as possible."

"These days, everybody wants to live as well as possible."

"I want a flashy car and a swimming pool like everyone else."

"Of course, the money matters—I've a family and mortgage to support."

"Look at the guys at the top—they're raking it in."

"I like to go on expensive holidays, so I work extra hard because it can make the difference to which hotel I stay at."

"Some people pretend they're not in it for the money—bull!"

Associated Unwritten Rules

M11 Conform to profile of business-oriented ambitious achiever

"We are full of ambitious clones."

"Your whole profile has to be focused on 'business orientation.'"

"Some people are definitely good at acting."

"Harvard MBAs are gods and you get kudos from the business game."

"Why work when you can hold meetings?"

"You get a pat on the back only if you show that what you did fits the strategy."

"Be seen as a manager, not a leader."

"We are all supposed to be macho, aggressive men."

"Panic prestige: There is no prestige unless you have or create a panic so you can sort it all out."

"The sexier it is, the better; inventing new things is what gets rewarded."

"We are an organization of rampant shapers, full of energy and ideas, but short on implementers and finishers."

"We will go aggressively along the wrong path."

M12 Almost no one survives past 50

"The current goal is to survive until you're 50."

"There is a strong belief that none of us is going to make it past 45."

"All the grey hairs have gone."

"They really don't like you being in your late 40s around here."

"Youth, not experience, is valued."

"Everyone wants to be a young Bill Gates or Steve Jobs."

"There's the feeling that if you're losing your hair you're losing your I.Q."

"How can you be bright and imaginative if you're old?"

"Whatever people pretend, we all know that we have lost many good people."

"Everyone who is left is above standard, so to an extent it's now luck of the draw."

"No one feels safe."

M13 In your early 40s start planning an exit route if you're marketable

"The trick is to get out before you're pushed."

"If you have marketable skills, there's no problem."

"You mustn't leave it too late or you can't really plan your second career."

"Come your 40th birthday and you should start planning to get out of this place."

"About 40 is when it bites."

"40 to 45—that's the time."

"50 would be way too late."

"No one wants to outstay their welcome."

"You need to plan your exit route carefully, otherwise you'll have to rush it and that's when you lose out."

"If you're not marketable then you just hang on for as long as you can."

"If you're unmarketable, then you're caught between a rock and a hard place."

M21 Ensure each promotion is to another part of R&D

"Obviously, you have to keep moving around."

"There would be no point getting promoted and then carrying on working in the same area."

"I want to keep right on moving."

"You have to keep jumping to different parts of R&D."

"Job hopping throughout R&D is still the way to progress."

"We still see moving on as moving up."

"Management use job rotation as a means of injecting new ideas."

"You can rarely take over your boss's shoes directly."

"The actual work we do is fascinating, so we're always looking for new challenges."

"I love the inherent change in the career profile here."

"We have to flit from flower to flower."

"It's not that we're butterflies—it's just that we want to see the big picture."

M22 Avoid staying in a particular job too long

"If you stay in the same job for too long people start to point at you."

"People would think: 'I thought she was a high flyer but obviously not.'"

"Too much stability leads to stagnation."

"We're like sharks—we need to keep moving in order to breathe."

"Staying too long would destroy your career."

"I was told that if I wasn't willing to move then I was finished."

"X wanted to see his project through, but he felt under such pressure to take up the offer of promotion that he moved on. We all know that the project suffered as a result. The client wasn't very happy."

M24 Constantly keep your eyes open for your next job in R&D

"You have to keep your eyes open—everyone else is after the same job."

"You never stop looking—you never know where the next opportunity in R&D will come from."

"You develop a radar for sensing the next job."

"Always have your antenna up."

"You need a sensor grid across the whole of R&D."

"You have to have the instincts of a good tracker."

"Some people get so stuck into their current job that they miss what would have been a great opportunity."

"I never stop searching."

M31 Make sure your colleagues know your achievements

"In this place, if you do something well you shout about it."

"What's the point of succeeding if no one knows about it."

"Your colleagues judge you by what they hear about you."

"Everyone else publicizes their achievements, so if you don't then your peers assume you haven't achieved anything worth publicizing."

"If you have it—flaunt it!"

"Maximum kudos go to those who we hear have sold big."

"People want to be seen to sell."

"Have people think you have the Midas touch."

"Sell big cases and shout about it."

"People like to be seen as the big sellers."

"The heroes are those who sell the big projects."

M32 Don't worry too much about external profile

"At the end of the day, it's what your colleagues think that matters."

"X spent too much time building his profile outside and not enough time focusing on his colleagues—so he got eased out. It's a shame, because he was probably getting us some good publicity. But no one saw it like that."

"It may sound harsh, but clients really come second round here."

"A client might say someone was no good, but the person in question is safe if we all know that really he's a good guy."

"You really don't need to worry about the outside world very much."

"We are our own guardians of quality."

M41 Avoid doing the same type of work twice

"We sell brains not methodologies."

"Ultimately we sell expertise."

"The whole value of this place is its creativity."

"Our work is not susceptible to 'turning the handle.'"

"Why would anybody want to do the same type of work twice?"

"If I thought I would be forced to keep doing the same thing—then bye-bye GF."

"Of course, other people tackle the same sorts of problems that I did. That's what may result in a fresh approach."

"Don't try to stifle creativity."

"Occasionally we keep making the same mistakes, but I guess that's a necessary sacrifice."

"Bright people need to learn from their own mistakes."

M42 Be available at the right place at the right time

"Your whole future may hinge on being in your office when someone walks down the corridor looking for someone for their project."

"It's all very ad hoc."

"You have to make damned sure you're available when you're needed."

"You can't say: 'Sorry, I'm interested but I'm tied up on this project for the next six months.' They'll just go somewhere else."

"Grab it when it comes along."

"Opportunism is the unwritten rule of this game."

M51 Do the things that will increase your personal bonus

"There's never enough time in the day—so you tend to prioritize by what will make an impact on your wallet."

"People prioritize their activities based on the signals they receive from the reward system."

"The elaborate evaluation process gives an utterly spurious feeling of accuracy."

"We all blindly act according to an engineering formula for our contingent compensation."

"Incentive payments are felt to be sufficiently important that they are destroying teamwork."

"You do what is necessary."

"Do whatever is necessary to meet your quarterly target for hours billed to an external client."

"Your bonus depends only on billing."

"You're only really judged on the total billability of your group."

"The pressure from the time record to keep a certain percentage billability is very explicit."

"There's pressure to do as much billable work as you're willing to do."

"Unbillable time is thought to be a sin."

"The Monday morning discussions are really useful—but there's the feeling that they're not really an acceptable use of time."

"There's a myth that we're a team, that we're being managed—but believe me, if you're not billable you're made to feel that it's your own fault and it's sure as hell your personal bonus that suffers."

"If you help sell a job, you're doing it for a percentage of the sales credit."

"Sales is one notch down from billability."

"If you can—hold onto the lead into a new client."

"Lots of people mask their lead reports."

"There are frequent fights over leads."

"If people think someone else might muscle in on their lead then they write up the lead report in very nebulous terms so others don't recognize it for what it is."

"You can always protect your lead by marking it confidential."

"You can run up a very large selling cost and eat into the project budget, because the prospect doesn't get reallocated by the sale credit formula."

"Don't give away any more sales credit than you need to."

**M52 Don't worry too much about things that don't get
measured**

"You're only valued if you make lots of money for GF—full stop."

"The bar has been raised and it's only the numbers that count."

"Your contribution to GF is only as good as your last one to two months' billability."

"They're trying to manage by numbers."

"When push comes to shove you only really care about getting the best numbers possible."

"Numbers, numbers, numbers."

"The reports we get reinforce this emphasis."

"As soon as profitability drops down—so too do memos from above."

"They tell you the numbers have no more weight than other things, but everyone believes that they do."

Consequent Potentially Positive Side Effects for High Performance

M+1 Collegiate environment with constant cross-fertilization

"Let's face it, it's like still being on campus."

"It all adds up to this place being really dynamic."

"You tend to hear about all sorts of things."

"You're always working with new, interesting people."

"Like any other carousel—it's fun!"

M+2 Well rounded employees with clear focus on specified goals

"By the time you become a senior, you tend to know something about everything."

"You can put a senior guy anywhere, and they've probably been there already."

"You don't tend to get narrow people—they tend to get weeded out."

"Everyone has a broad perspective."

"Each of us knows what's important and goes after it."

Consequent Potentially Negative Side Effects for High Performance

M–1 Nobody tends to think strategically

"They don't realize that there are some important things to our business success that are not easily quantified"

"Why this constant focus only on numbers?"

"I am not a number—I am a free man!"

"You should minimize nonbillable, nonselling activities."

"Only sales and billability really count."

"Even though you have to do other things—billability of your group is still the only important criterion."

"There's an attitude that if you're not billable you're not contributing."

"Strategy—what strategy?"

"Our sort of business is too dynamic to think long term."

"To think long term would tie our hands behind our back."

"We need to remain free and responsive."

"How can you plan for something that is so uncertain?"

M–2 Chronic short-termism

"Down deep, we are not very patient."

"If something doesn't work at once then we never try it again."

"We try out some good ideas, then if they're not a major success we revert to the old ways of doing things."

"We'll often try something only once. We place too much stock in the first time we do something."

"We're so short term we can't possibly make investments in training or products or the future generally."

"We have too short a horizon for profitability."

"My concern is that keeping to the numbers' targets and the short term view of our profitability can compromise the work we're doing."

"Two quarters below target and there's a salary/hiring freeze."

"Of course, some managers think medium term—they think as far as the end of the quarter!"

M–3   No one is concerned about long-term consequences of their (in)action

"You can never tell what's going to happen after you move on."

"You can't really measure your impact once you've changed roles."

"There's a lack both of significant rewards and of demonstrably successful role models for worrying about long-term consequences of what you do or don't do."

"Like we tell our clients: 'What gets measured gets managed.' We don't measure, reward, or manage long term."

"We need to let people recognize the successes or failures of their past."

"Management has to show the pattern of leadership to support such a new idea."

"The top need to demonstrate through actions that long-term consequences of what we do is relevant."

"It must be in a person's self interest."

"There's absolutely no incentive to worry."

"Other companies make awards to recognize things like strategic initiatives that finally made good—why don't we?"

"We need some very credible examples to force the issue—find GF successes and hold up role models."

"We need to have a mechanism for people to aspire to and look up to heroes."

"Management must evaluate these contributions and genuinely include them in performance reviews."

"Come on! The reality is that your past never catches up with you."

"I've got more than enough to concentrate on now without keeping track of what happened in the past."

"Yes, some things did go wrong after I left, but I sincerely believe that in each case it was the fault of my successor."

"Why worry?"

M-4 Self-fulfilling prophesy that employees over 50 are unproductive

"Of course we don't have any good guys over 50—they all leave!"

"All the good ones leave in their 40s."

"It's only the ones we don't really want that stay."

"If the outside world doesn't want them—neither do we."

"We've got caught up in a vicious spiral."

"It's become self-fulfilling."

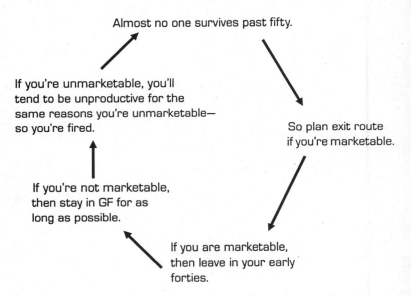

Almost no one survives past fifty.

If you're unmarketable, you'll tend to be unproductive for the same reasons you're unmarketable—so you're fired.

So plan exit route if you're marketable.

If you're not marketable, then stay in GF for as long as possible.

If you are marketable, then leave in your early forties.

M-5 Poor relationships with clients

"Clients are seen as a means to an end."

"The more senior we get, the more we focus on GF rather than clients."

"You're rewarded for focusing on internal affairs."

"We spend far too much time focusing on trash (that is, internal administration)."

"There's an imbalance in our preoccupation with internal activities."

"We're very bad at understanding client concerns."

"Even our sales techniques tend to make us focus only on the shorter term issues of our clients."

"We have a poor record of recognizing our clients' needs."

"Our clients need us to have a long-term vision, but who has it?"

"How can you network with clients properly when you're moving around all the time?"

"Job hopping has led to a real lack of ability to service our clients."

"We need to have much more continuity with our clients; relationships are critical."

"Clients want to see the same faces, but we keep changing them."

"We've got it all wrong, you can learn a client-specific technology within six months but you can't inherit relationships."

"These days, clients expect more."

"It was OK in the past."

"The days of clients beating a path to our door are over."

"Clients are getting fed up—and I don't blame them."

"We can't carry on like this much longer."

"Our main competitors are far more responsive and build far better relationships."

"We are surviving on our reputation."

"We have got to do something."

Rules and Side Effects with Supporting Quotes: Enablers

Period: Current   **Grade:** Intermediate   **Category:** NYHQ

N.B. Unwritten rules can, in principle, **all** be beneficial, although side effects and conflicts may create barriers to high performance.

Enablers

E1   The Ghee family and functional chiefs (for firing)

"If the family take a dislike to you—you're dead meat."

"The ultimate law around here is the family."

"Be in no doubt—we're all the servants of the family to be disposed of as and when they see fit."

"They're like benevolent dictators, with the power of life and death."

"The functional chiefs have the day-to-day power over whether you leave or stay."

"The family usually listens to the advice of the functional chiefs on who should go."

E2   The Ghee family (for rapid promotion)

"You need a sponsor in the family if you're going to fly fast and high."

"In GF, it's 'jobs for the boys' as far as the family is concerned."

"It's who you know that counts."

"Electronic job posting is a joke, it's all fixed behind the scenes."

"If it says 'preferred candidate,' don't waste time applying."

"It's just not a level playing field."

"I was told I was good at networking but needed exposure to the family."

"There's a tendency to attend any family meeting in strong preference to any other meetings."

"The thrusting elite like the sound of their voices intermingling with those of the family."

E3   Peers (for respect)

"To gain respect you need to maintain your reputation with your peers."

"People are vindictive if you make a mistake."

"You end up not being trusted."

"The rumor mill is as strong as ever, even in top management; the facts don't matter."

"Your colleagues don't consider working from home as real work."

"Peer pressure is very strong."

E4   Functional chiefs (for exciting work)

"At the end of the day it's your function head that dictates what you do."

"If the functional chief isn't impressed by you, you'll be bored to tears until he is."

"X is a good guy, but he just doesn't get on with his (functional) chief, so he's doomed to working like a technician."

"If you're the blue eyed boy then you get brilliant work."

"Stay on the right side of the function and you'll be kept at the cutting edge of technology."

E5   Your line boss and your boss's boss (for individual bonus)

"After two months in the company I think that the most important people that affect my bonus are A (boss) and B (boss's boss)—nobody's told me, but that's the way I see it."

"Your boss is not enough."

"It ultimately doesn't matter what your boss thinks provided you've got his boss in your pocket."

"The people to lobby are those in a direct line to you getting approval for a big bonus."

"To get a fat bonus you need to persuade your boss and his boss."

"In many ways your boss's boss is the most important person to you bonus-wise."

"You're always trying to impress two levels away."

"It's a function of our organization structure—you need to have profile with those that count."

"Our hierarchy is sufficiently shallow that you don't have to go further than your boss's boss."

"You might take your boss's job—so it's his boss that you have to worry about."

Associated Unwritten Rules

E01   Never let anyone see you fail

"You dare not let people see you get it wrong because of what they will think."

"You're still not allowed to be associated with failure."

"Don't surprise people."

"If people see you make one mistake, that's it."

"These days, if you make a mistake, you're not forgiven."

"We're rather like Hollywood—we love successes but we turn our back on people when we see them on the way down."

"It's all to do with people's attitudes."

"It's psycho-logic rather than logic."

"Crowd dynamics. What once was a cheering group turns into a lynch mob."

"X was at the top of the tree, then one failure and everyone ruled him off."

"If you do screw up you really have to hide it."

"If people hear what went wrong it can have a disproportionate impact."

"Never let them see you fail."

"Never let your boss see you make a mistake."

"Never let your colleagues see you fouled up."

"Hide any screw ups from the functional chiefs."

"Never, never, ever let the family even think that you might possibly have once casually even thought about failing."

E11   Never get on the wrong side of the family

"To err is human; to forgive is the prerogative of the family."

"It is never worth crossing the family, X did and look what happened to him."

"Whatever you do, you must never paint yourself into a corner with respect to the family."

"Always give yourself a let-out."

"Whatever they ask, you cannot risk refusing."

"It's like dealing with a petulant despot."

"You have to smile and grit your teeth."

"However much you disagree, it's just not worth it."

E12 Never displease the functional chiefs

"We still have a few of the old style managers in the functions."

"Treat them like the power behind the throne and you won't go far wrong."

"No one who one of the chiefs liked has ever been fired—only sidelined."

"A few have rebelled but they never got away with it."

"Keep in their good books."

"Pity the poor S.O.B. who gets caught in having to choose between displeasing the family or one of the chiefs. He'd probably commit hari-kari just to avoid having to choose."

E21 Do everything to join the in crowd

"People only share good jobs with their friends."

"There's tremendous cronyism."

"You get the best leads if you're in favor."

"If you're not part of the inner circle you only get scraps."

"You often have to give away 5- to 10-percent sales credit to appease someone who wasn't really involved."

E22 Nothing is more important than pleasing the family

"It's a no brainer."

"Everybody knows it."

"It's tattooed onto your chest when your join the firm."

"I'm sure that people come back from the grave for them sometimes."

"The family have the cleanest backsides in New York, because of all the kissing."

E31 Earn your club membership by proving your loyalty

"Be seen as loyal to the club."

"You've got to be a good corporate citizen as far as your peers are concerned."

"You show your loyalty to the club by sacrifice."

"You've got to work blood hours just like your colleagues."

"It varies a lot by section, but most people are working longer days."

"These days you have to consistently work long hours."

"It's too easy to work yourself to death in this organization."

"I want to have a life outside GF."

"Pity your chances if you're not willing to be away from home a lot."

"You have to be seen to put work before family."

"Sacrifice your private life."

"I feel guilty if I leave at 7 to see my kids."

"We should involve family more, but no one does."

"You can't afford to become a mother until you're already a success."

E32 Socialize with colleagues out of work time

"It's the done things for people to get together outside work."

"You can get a lot of wheels oiled by socializing."

"People tend to go out with their peers rather than those above or below them."

"We're rather Japanese in this regard."

"If someone consistently didn't want to get involved with the rest of us, I guess we'd feel he wasn't part of the team and we'd act accordingly."

"It's like a club—we work together so we play together."

E41 Keep in constant touch with your function

"You have to maintain your profile with your technical function."

"We have all the old technical bias of the defense work holding us back."

"Technicians love being technicians, it's a job in its own right."

"If you don't keep in constant touch with your function then you really risk being forgotten when it comes to the next exciting project."

"You have to keep a constant profile with them."

"Make sure you're never too far from their thoughts."

E51 Keep your line boss and your boss's boss happy

"It's the same throughout R&D—manage upwards two or three levels."

"Pleasing the boss has now superseded pleasing the client."

"The higher you can go the better, but you need to appease your boss's envy by tossing him the occasional bone."

"It was always there, but now it's more overt."

"You are rewarded for making your boss happy, his boss happy, and his boss happy; that's not professional, it's political—but it's also practical."

"We're afraid to shake the tree in terms of challenging the 'pleasing the boss' syndrome."

"Some people pretend it isn't there."

E53 Stand out from the crowd, but not too much

"Everything is focused on the individual rather than the team."

"You have to stand out from the crowd."

"If you submerge your ego and become a genuine team player, then it's the other guy that gets the rewards."

"There are no rewards for being a faceless individual."

"If you don't stand out you won't be noticed."

"You have to get profile—otherwise who will know that you're valuable?"

"Then again, you don't want to stand out too far."

"It all has to be very civilized—not too pushy."

"No one wants to stand out so far that they find themselves standing on a limb that's about to fall off."

"You don't want to take an extreme position and then find that you're the only one."

"Standing out is a two-edged sword—you get everyone's attention but therefore they'll see every slip and every mistake."

"We give people enough rope to climb to the next peak or else to hang themselves."

Consequent Potentially Positive Side Effects for High Performance

E+1 Mutually supportive environment

"Generally everybody supports everybody else."

"Because every one has to worry about what everyone else thinks, it has a beneficial impact."

"It can feel like a very supportive environment."

"If you genuinely want help you can usually get it."

"Provided you haven't burnt your bridges people will help you."

"We all need each other."

"I don't know whether it's a symbiotic relationship or a mutually parasitic relationship—either way we all tend to depend on each other in one way or another."

E+2 Possible to get occasional major job through extremely fast "as favor"

"One of the benefits of the system is that in an emergency you can get something through quickly."

"You can't get away with it very often, but you can get everyone to move into overdrive."

"On the X project, **everyone** pulled together—that was great."

"On occasion, everyone is doing everyone else the same favor."

"Rarely, we act like a massive extended family to the family, and do whatever is necessary."

Consequent Potentially Negative Side Effects for High Performance

E–1 Long lead times are caused by poor cross-company cooperation

"There's an arrogance that people can't believe that someone else has come up with a good idea that it's not necessary to improve."

"People tend to be very cynical."

"It's become a very whining culture."

"Intellectual pride fights cross-company cooperation."

"NIH was invented here in GF, New York!"

"People reject working with other parts of R&D because they don't know enough about why a client would want them to."

"We need a way to get people to give time to others' ideas without negative criticism."

"The toughest sell is to your colleagues."

"No one wants to risk ridicule."

"People are inhibited in sharing half-baked ideas."

"Why bother trying to persuade others—just use it for your own ends."

"We always need the perfect solution."

"We seek perfection."

"When we appear before a client our culture says we must have the answer—it's not right to admit we don't have it all thought out yet."

"All of this adds up to chronic lead times."

"Everything always takes so long."

"Because of all this attitude everything takes forever."

"If people would only genuinely cooperate we could halve lead times."

"Everything's taking far too long."

"It's a sad joke."

E-2 Clients find solutions solidly professional but unexciting

"Who's going to take a personal risk in an organization like this?"

"The trick is to be steadfastly professional but not take any unnecessary risks."

"It's just not worth coming up with something revolutionary."

"People don't realize that to be truly imaginative you have to go out on a limb."

"No one can fault us on quality, but it's that undefinable element that's missing."

"These days you would never call our stuff exciting."

"We've turned into boring old professionals."

"People seem to think there's something somehow not quite right about being exciting."

"They talk about glitz as if that's something that's beneath us."

"We're supposed to be ever so respectable."

"People equate quality with boringness."

"You know, it's sad—I think old Robert Ghee was a bit of a huckster. He had panache. He once installed gold plated Louis XV handles throughout the personal radio studio we built for the King of Siam. I bet he'd be disappointed with the sort of stuff we deliver today."

E-3 Inability to leverage senior skills

"No one ever wants to delegate."

"People want to be in charge and be seen to be in charge."

"Nobody wants to do the same sort of thing twice, so it always needs the most experienced person available to run the show."

"Everyone is always so busy being seen that they can't spend the time training others to do what they do. Anyway, they wouldn't want other people to do what they do!"

"You have to keep so many people happy at the same time in this organization, that no one is going to give up responsibility to someone else."

"You can delegate responsibility, but it's still your neck on the block if something goes wrong."

"If I'm going to be blown out of the water, I'd rather that it was all my fault than that I had that awful feeling that if only I'd taken care of things myself then maybe none of this would have happened."

"Why would we want to leverage senior skills anyway?"

E-4   Voice mail overload saturating everybody

"Voice mail has been a gift from heaven for getting noticed."

"It's great—you can accidentally bump into 10 people in the corridors of the voice mail system in less than a minute."

"You can copy people that you would never otherwise meet."

"It lets you pass on information that you would never want to put in a memo because that would make it seem too formal."

"If in doubt, leave a voice mail—that way you're protected."

"Always cover your back by leaving a voice mail."

"I waste up to an hour a day listening to the bloody voice mail."

"I hate voice mail more than anything in the whole world apart from taxes."

Rules and Side Effects with Supporting Quotes: Triggers

Period: Current   **Grade:** Intermediate   **Category:** NYHQ

N.B. Unwritten rules can, in principle, **all** be beneficial, although side effects and conflicts may create barriers to high performance.

Triggers

T1   Correct profile (to avoid being fired)

"Conform to the profile of the ideal GFer if you want to be safe."

"You have to look right if you want to avoid the chop."

"Conform and prosper!"

"Nobody says anything, but you suddenly notice that most of the people that were willing to stand out of line aren't here any more."

"Don't criticize."

"We've had our own cultural revolution like in China."

"You really have to fit in if you're to be protected from the firing squad."

"There's an ideal GFer, and that's what you need to be."

T2   Perceived value to firm (for family)

"News of bad performance travels quickly."

"Once bitten twice shy—they don't support someone again."

"They start talking of one rotten apple spoiling the barrel."

"Some people get three chances—others they write off first time."

"Some people are destroyed by one mistake."

"The family judges everybody by what value they bring to the firm."

"If the family doesn't believe you can add value to the firm, then you can't add any value. It's a Catch 22."

T3 Perceived profile (by peers)

"You've got to be seen in the right light by your peers."

"Work is mostly going to come from other GFers; do it well and knowledge of you will spread through the network."

"Lots of communication is by rumor."

"You need to be known—not necessarily by all your peers—but you need to be known and in the right way."

"Your colleagues like to see you working as hard as they are."

"Be seen to be here 12 hours a day and that helps."

"If you're only here 8 until 5:30, you must be doing something wrong."

"There is too much kudos for working after hours."

"There's a perception that if you can deliver in 40 hours, you're under employed."

T4 Technical competence (for functional chiefs)

"You need to be seen as valuable by the functional chiefs—and they value technical competence."

"It's all about marketability, inside **and** eventually outside GF."

"If you're average on the technical competency front, you're out."

"Provided you're seen as a true 'techie' you're OK."

"The functional chiefs love people who look like them."

T5 Current financial performance of your current group (for line boss)

"Your boss looks at your personal financials."

"It's all about profit and loss."

"Your line boss is really only interested in your P&L."

"Keeping up your quarterlies is all your boss wants."

"Our line bosses are measured on the P&L of their group—so what do you think they pressurize us on?"

"They get pressure from above to get the best financial performance possible, so they pass that pressure on to us."

Associated Unwritten Rules

TO1 Build credit with all key influencers and power brokers

"There's a lot of tit-for-tat."

"It's all about quid pro quo."

"Some people don't realize that you need to play chips—build credit that in due course you can cash in."

"You have to be able to do people favors so you can collect later."

"I think of it as exchanging chits."

"Did you ever see the film "The Godfather"?"

"You can keep people above you happy by giving them some token sales credit—particularly if they don't deserve it."

"Above all else you've got to superplease the folks who count."

"You need exposure to the right people so you can do them favors."

"You need to know the key people other than your boss and boss's boss."

"You have to know how to promote yourself."

"Most people are looking upwards to influencers and forget about those below."

"If someone at the top of the company gives something his attention then it's likely to happen."

"That's why you have to participate in internal initiatives."

"You need to have X on your side, so you need to help X out first."

"If Y doesn't support an idea it's unlikely anything will happen. That's why everyone is always so helpful when Y wants something."

"It's all a game of transactional politics."

TO2 **Play safe**

"Keep your head down."

"Don't stick you head out too far."

"It's not safe to sit in a meeting and say: 'I think this is a load of crap.'"

"We are supposed to 'Boldly go where no man has gone before.' The unwritten ending is: '... but if you go even slightly wrong, you'll come to harm.'"

"CYA is the watchword—we all do it."

"Hide behind collective decisions."

"Know the limits of your freedom."

"Some people avoid making decisions and so minimize any risk of making mistakes."

"Personal risk taking is no longer in our culture—it used to be."

"Try to avoid being the accountable person."

"The GF business philosophy is: Play safe, even if it costs money."

"We have not even started to move to a learning organization."

"Learning organization—very funny. How the heck can you learn if you can't make mistakes?"

"For the last year we've been talking about becoming a learning organization—what a joke."

"All we've learned is how to play safe even better than before."

"People don't believe that they're free to take risks; the words are there but they are for 'respect for the American family.'"

T11 Avoid leaving the United States

"GF personnel don't want to move from New York Headquarters."

"Out of sight, out of mind."

"You have to remain visible within GF."

"You don't want to be away from New York for too long."

"Intermediates and juniors have to be seen in New York."

"He didn't get his directorship because he wasn't generally well known."

"There are very few success models who went abroad and did well."

"People are scared stiff about repatriation."

"Now is not a good time to be away from the Big Apple."

"You must not lose your link to a sponsor."

"Things are moving too fast to be absent."

"Better an intermediate than a senior with no job in three years."

"You will come back in a coffin."

"People are worrying they'll come back in a body bag."

"Many of the new overseas posts are not very pleasant anyway."

"The ultimate dilemma: being a reasonably ambitious intermediate and being offered a post overseas!"

T12 Declare ambition

"You have to offer yourself as mobile and willing to go overseas. You just hope that they don't take you at your word."

"Perceived commitment is important; make the right noises and work long hours."

"The whole system is based on the ridiculous assumption that everyone wants to climb to the top of the organization."

"You can't say that you're not ambitious or you'll not be given the chance to reach the level you want."

"Many people certainly don't aspire to the pressure of a senior job."

"Once you get above intermediate, you're in the spotlight, so maybe it's better to avoid it."

"These days, many people simply don't want to move around every two years."

"The system can't cope with the very competent but not overtly ambitious high performer."

T13 Espouse team orientation

"We don't take our juniors to meetings."

"You don't indicate other people's contributions to a memo that goes out under your own signature."

"Status symbols are important."

"The team leader gets the glory."

"Always 'I did this' or 'My team did this,' never 'We.'"

"Individual spot bonuses are insidious and divisive."

"Be seen to network."

"The visibly successful networker can, and will, prosper."

"It's alright being in a team, provided you can be the leader."

T14 Never sponsor anything alcoholic to the family

"Things have changed since the days of Robert Sr. It's as if they weren't very proud of their roots."

"I don't know what's wrong with the word 'alcohol' but I do know it gets you pickled."

"X just mentioned that the new components cleaning system was alcohol-based and the whole room went very quiet."

"It's rumored that they've all gone teetotal."

"For a while, everybody started using the chemical term 'Ethanol' as a substitute for the 'A word'—but then the family cottoned on."

"I once had to give the family a 30-minute presentation about the alcohol recovery plant that we still have in Scotland. I kept referring to C_2H_5OH, and I think I got away with it."

"The joke about 'Shaken, not stirred' went down very badly."

T15 Never appear too loyal to line managers in front of functional chiefs

"It can all get very difficult—you need to keep your line boss happy but you **really** need to keep you functional chief happy. Ideally you sit on the fence."

"You can't appear too loyal to your line manager in front of your function—you'd be cutting yourself off."

"If push comes to shove you have to side with the function."

"The way you do it is to side with your line boss in public but let the function know before hand that you're only doing it to keep your boss happy. They understand that."

"It's all a question of the games people play."

"The functions know how the game is played."

"Sometimes you have to agree to one thing but do the other."

"It's naive if someone sets up a meeting with your boss and function head in the same room—you can't get any real decision. The safe route is never to let it come to that."

T21 Be associated with the family's pet projects

"At any given time the family has a pet project—so that's what you get involved with."

"First it was leadtime, then it was quality, then it was vision, now it's reengineering—for which read downsizing—and I guess if you guys get your way the next thing'll be unwritten rules."

"There's nothing that does you more good than being involved in one of the family schemes."

"It kills so many birds with the one stone."

"Do whatever is needed to get involved."

T22 Give high-profile presentations and feedback

"In the past, good presentation skills were all-important; things improved for a while but now they are reverting."

"If in doubt, give a flashy presentation."

"Most managers can't see past the viewgraphs."

"The flashier the better."

"It's all to do with profile."

"The greatest opportunity comes from being asked to present in the main boardroom—that has electronically generated backprojection and allows for all sorts of slow dissolves and special effects."

"Whatever you get involved in, aim to be the one who feeds back the results."

"The more important the audience, the better."

"You can offer to send them a copy of the report, which will take you a few seconds, or you can offer to give them a rerun of the presentation, which will take a minimum of a few hours preparation. Which do you think you always choose?"

T23 Do the family unsolicited favors

"We are always on the lookout for how to do the family a favor."

"If you do something for the family that they didn't even ask for—and they like it—you're a star."

"X made it to the top because he could anticipate what the family would want. As soon as they asked for it he was ready. Very clever guy."

"They are this company, so when you help them you help everybody—not least yourself."

"They can be very generous to those who please them."

"They have their favorites who suck up to them like their lives depended on it. Thinking about it, their lives probably do depend on it."

T31 Don't be seen to be egocentric

"You can't get away with being too selfish."

"You have to be made a star by others—if people think you want it too much they get envious and want to stop you."

"Remember, we value our collegiate atmosphere, so no one has the right to stand above anyone else."

"You can get away with it provided that no one thinks you want it."

"X was thought to have too great an ego and he was ostracized."

"It's all to do with human nature."

"The best you should aim for is to be first among equals."

T32 Always appear helpful to your colleagues

"You have to be nice to your peers."

"Be a people person."

"Strive for consensus."

"You've got to get along with others."

"Disagree agreeably."

"You can get away with being an S.O.B., but only if you're a highly successful S.O.B."

T41 Be seen as an expert

"The functions want you to be expert in their eyes."

"Be known for quality expertise."

"People are always described as 'the expert on so-and-so."

"You have to be 'expert.'"

"Expert this, expert that."

"People love being experts."

"We all want to be seen as 'expert.'"

"When you want to flatter someone you call them an expert."

"You introduce someone as an expert on whatever they do."

"Meet your commitments as far as the functions are concerned."

"Be seen as a good professional."

"Have a professional reputation."

"You need to be seen as professional in your chosen expertise."

T51 Protect your own turf

"The trick is to stake your turf."

"Some groups are very turfy."

"Everybody's protecting their own patch."

"Grab an area and call it your own."

"Pull in people around you."

"Build a successful empire."

"People protect their narrow areas of expertise like mad."

"There's lots of turfiness between units—even within units."

"Of course there's still a great deal of turfiness."

"Turf battles continue."

"Although general turfiness has diminished, there are still management battles going on."

"Financial resource sharing is still not good."

"Management power struggles are a worry."

"Everyone is jockeying for position."

T52 Keep your quarterlies up

"Do whatever necessary to keep your quarterlies on target."

"It's common sense."

"All the signals are to focus on the quarterlies."

"People play all sorts of games to keep on target."

"If you've had a good quarter, you don't bother to book the new work until next quarter."

"You have to try to squirrel away a reserve that nobody knows about."

"Keep your quarterlies on track and you tend to be left alone."

T53 Get contracts for your own group now

"There's tremendous pressure from above to **get contracts**."

"The trouble is that you're not rewarded for deciding to let a client 'go fallow' for a while, even if that's the best business decision."

"I was told: You're not allowed to plan for failure."

"Play the macho businessman."

"Think bigger the more ambitious you are."

"Sacrifice the future for the present."

"Why worry about future contracts when you'll be long gone?"

"The only rewards are for the here and now."

"No one ever got a bonus based on promises."

"Even if you did do something that would build into a juicy contract in three or four years time it's your successor—or maybe even his successor—that will benefit from all your hard work. Meanwhile, you've wasted time you could otherwise have spent getting results that would benefit you. It would be a stupid thing to do—and I don't know of anyone who does."

Consequent Potentially Positive Side Effects for High Performance

None mentioned.

Consequent Potentially Negative Side Effects for High Performance

T–1 Teamwork does not happen

"Don't waste time on cross-company activities between different sections of R&D."

"There's no reason to spend time on multiunit or multisection issues, and there's a positive penalty to doing things of benefit to more than one directorate."

"Everything is fighting corporate teamwork."

"If we can possibly do it within our group, we don't work with others."

"We keep claiming that some of their activities are really ours."

"We tend to keep ourselves to ourselves."

"We claim that we differentiate ourselves from our competitors because we are international, but we act like separate companies."

"Let's face it, genuine teamwork in this company just doesn't get you anywhere."

"The inability to be one GF is a pathetic indictment."

T–2 Only the best, the worst, or the over-40s are willing to go abroad

"If you don't think you will survive anyway, enjoy yourself abroad for your last three years in GF."

"Only the stars and the poorer performers are willing to go."

"The elite feel safe about coming back, but some of them have been lost."

"Going to foreign countries is less acceptable now."

"If you've planned your exit route then it doesn't matter if you go abroad."

"If you're going to leave anyway, you go abroad because then you may be lucky and pick up the redundancy package that you couldn't get if you resigned."

"It's become a form of euthanasia."

"The trouble is that as a result it's almost impossible to get the right people to go."

"How will we find good people to staff the X, Y, and Z projects?"

T–3 Inadequate diversity

"Diversity is hardly tolerated; it's very difficult if you're female, belong to an ethnic minority, have the wrong profile, joined late, developed late, or are a maverick."

"Sexist and racist attitudes are very common."

"It is an unwritten rule to be white and male."

"My wife looks at us and says we all look exactly the same."

"Surround yourself with like minded (former) colleagues."

"Managers select their friends from the past."

"Better the beast you know ... "

"Technical and commercial ability are rewarded, not leadership."

"There's a belief that someone who is a good technical person will be a good manager, but it doesn't work!"

"To be a manager, you need to prove you're technically smart."

"We're looking for a Ph.D. from MIT; a degree from outside the United States is worse than no degree at all!"

"There's an identikit GF person."

"GF man: intellectual, mid-30s, dark and intense."

"We all thought "internationalization" was a good idea; but it turned out just to mean U.S. citizens flying around on planes."

"There's a business risk in trusting locals."

"We're told that foreign degrees aren't good enough. So how many ethnic minorities have you seen in GF **from U.S. universities**?"

"Hire the person who fits."

"HR are the worst; they avoid risk by maintaining the status quo."

"Males fear equal opportunities; they worry that a woman can climb a grade easier than they can."

"We're really missing a trick by not encouraging diversity."

"Good team work is supposed to be all about benefiting from diversity, and we're useless at it."

"We should recognize and encourage greater diversity."

"It's unreasonable to think everyone should be good at everything."

"There's a uniform expectation that all staff members must do everything."

"We all have to be the same profile."

"There's very little diversity tolerated any more."

"We're all supposed to be the same."

"You don't make friends by being exceptional."

"Not everybody is good at everything—we need to recognize differ-ent needs and skill sets."

"We desperately need diversity."

"We won't bring in someone unless they look like they'll be good at everything—the whole profile is self perpetuated."

"There's a cookie cutter mentality."

"We have a cookie cutter approach to choosing people."

"We need to not use the cookie cutter approach to staff selection."

"We might not be hiring the right kind of creative people."

"We may not be hiring or keeping enough mavericks—we need them."

"The trouble is, I don't ever see us changing."

T–4   Standards, rigor, and corporate memory have all gone down.

"Why think on a 5-year horizon? So we drop the ball!"

"The apparent need to job hop destroys the patience we really need."

"There's a strong bias to action **now**, but these days we really need a more considered approach."

"Information is power, so hang onto it."

"There's a lot of plagiarism going on."

"Oh yes, communication has dramatically improved, but that doesn't mean people have stopped hiding information."

"Hold onto a report until you've got it finalized; don't seek opinions early."

"Sometimes you only find out something valuable too late, and you wonder why nobody mentioned it."

"When people hide information, it's for political reasons not busi-ness reasons; they want to make sure that it's they who shine."

"People hang onto information to protect their position."

"With the tremendous pressure to perform, people keep quiet about a discovery because they don't want anyone to steal their thunder."

"They kept quiet about the breakthrough and did not involve us when they should have."

"Ego-tripping leads some groups not to ask for help."

"There is an attitude from some that they don't need any advice."

"We're managed by press release."

"We made the press release then tried to get the patent to match it."

"Bright young things have become a danger."

"People are making contracts who do not even understand basic business principles."

"There's a definite loss of rigor."

"There's lots of activity without tight focus or measurement of outcome."

"There's so much pressure to make a breakthrough."

"People are skimping under pressure."

"Errors are creeping in from overwork; it's happened to me."

"People already work after hours as standard, so there's no capacity to cope with genuine major panics."

"We're **really** storing up problems for the future."

END FILE

Boston, March 1994

Dear Rulebuster,

You are now approaching the end of The Rulebuster's Guide. There isn't much more that I can do to help you. From now on it's largely up to you.

Before I close, though, let me offer a few insights about the report you've just read. Firstly, although Ghee Formulates {an anagram, by the way} appears fictitious, it's actually a _composite_ *report based on authentic appraisals. Different aspects of the analysis bear striking resemblances to genuine companies. Secondly, each of the quotable quotes to support the various rules and side effects is real. Somebody, somewhere, actually made each of those statements as part of an unwritten rules analysis. And I heard them say it. What's more, they said it in support of the rules and side effects that the quotes are attached to here. Thirdly, don't worry too much about the length of the report. Although you'll sometimes need to go into that much detail, you can often get away with a report half the length.*

Finally, always remember that the report itself is just a means to an end for top management to understand what's going on and so make the changes necessary to break through the barriers to change. Draw hope from the fact that each of the real world companies on which the Ghee Formulates report is based _did_ *manage to do something. They broke the stranglehold of their unwritten rules.* _That_ *is the ultimate deliverable of the true Rulebuster ...*

And so, let me end.

To each of you, the very best of luck in breaking the rules!